Cognac

By the same author

Lafite: The Story of Château Lafite-Rothschild

Cognac

Cyril Ray

STEIN AND DAY/*Publishers*/New York

First published in the United States in 1974
Copyright © 1973 by Cyril Ray
Library of Congress Catalog Card No. 73-81324
All rights reserved
Printed in the United States of America
Stein and Day/*Publishers*/Scarborough House, Briarcliff Manor, N.Y. 10510
ISBN 0-8128-1617-X

To

HAL and NAN MILNER-GULLAND

—only a book, not a bottle,

but with

gratitude and affection

CONTENTS

vii

Contents

ILLUSTRATIONS

Illustrations

NOTE: The line drawings of brandy glasses on page 135 were kindly executed by Mr Michael Broadbent of Christie's; all chapter-headings and decorative tail-pieces are from Bertall's *La Vigne: Voyage autour des Vins de France*, as they were for my books on Lafite and Bollinger. Bertall's engagingly light-hearted book was published in Paris in 1878, and his material was gathered at just about the time that the phylloxera reached the vineyards of the Charentes. Indeed, the drawings of the 'millionaire of the Cognac country' on page 150 and of the American's revenge on page 147 are highly relevant to this period: the small wine-grower of the Charentes was passing rich before the phylloxera struck in about 1876, and that disaster, which came from America, was the revenge taken for the conquest of the United States—perhaps for the corruption of the redskin?—by cognac.

Introduction

This book is an act of piety.

After I had written, and had had published, monographs (in no way initiated or sponsored by the firms concerned) on a noble claret, Lafite, and on a great champagne, Bollinger, it seemed obvious not only to various good friends, mere acquaintances, and correspondents whom I had never met, but also to my publisher and—at first—to me that my next task must be to write about another famous individual wine or individual wine-growing property.

'Where will he turn up next,' mused Mr Edmund Penning-Rowsell, at the end of a generous review of *Bollinger* in the *Financial Times*, 'at Château d'Yquem, Schloss Johannisberg or in Taylor's lodge at Oporto?'

These three very names had indeed been much in my publisher's mind and mine, along with those of the Domaine de la Romanée-Conti and the Clos de Vougeot. We had debated—and doubted—whether Herr Pruem's Sonnenuhr vineyard at Wehlen was as well-known to potential book-buyers as those of the

Bernkasteler Doktor (my publisher, quite properly, demanding a name, as title, well-known enough to be beckoning in a bookshop) and had turned our minds to life-enhancing liquors other than wine—arguing Guinness against Pilsner, and quoting obscure Scottish poets to each other in support of the Glenlivet.

But the more I lay awake at nights, savouring such palate-tickling problems, the more I realized that my duty lay elsewhere.

I had written about the wine that, more than any other, I love to drink before what I hope will be a good dinner. I had chosen Bollinger, as the archetypal champagne.

I had written about the wine without which as an accompaniment, either to main course or to cheese, no dinner is to me as good as all that. Lafite stood for claret.

Surely, I thought, having paid my modest tribute to champagne as a preliminary and to claret as an accompaniment, the next step must be to write about what must, for me, follow a good dinner.

No, not port.

I respect port. I am fascinated by the part that it has played in English social life, and in writing this I think not only of the historical reason why we drink our Hanoverian monarch's health in port (instead of a Stuart's in claret) and not only of vintage port in senior common rooms but also of port-and-lemon in the boozer.

I have been entertained royally in that dignified example of English Georgian architecture *in partibus infidelium*, the Factory House in Oporto and, by the same hospitable heads of port houses, in their lonely *quintas* up the wild valley of the Douro. I consider that one of the most readable of recent books on any wine in English is Sarah Bradford's *The Englishman's Wine*, which is all about port.

And yet port is not my tipple—not even the fine old tawnies of which those Oporto custodians of old English customs taught me (while I was a temporary resident, indeed, of the Oporto Cricket Club) to be, if not a passionate lover, at any rate a platonic admirer.

I confessed in the first book about wine I ever wrote (and I have no scruples about repeating myself by quoting from it here, because no one ever read it) that port and sherry and madeira are

'wines that I respect and am interested in, and in which I think I can see, academically, what other people see emotionally, if emotionally is the word, but that I do not care a great deal about, myself. What I see in port is rather what a male homosexual sees in a beautiful and beautifully turned-out young woman. It interests, but it does not stir me.'

Not port then, and not an after-dinner sherry or madeira.

Not liqueurs, either, though there are infrequent occasions, perhaps because my diet at the time has been for too long too short of sugar, when I love to toy with those pretty little liquid sweetmeats, glowing with colour like slivers of stained glass.

Not even one of those dry, fragrant *alcools blancs*, though calvados in Normandy and kirsch or quetsch or mirabelle in Alsace have crowned many a memorable meal; not even old Irish whiskey or Highland malt, though these in their time have done more than Milton can. . . . Certainly not *marc*, certainly not *grappa*, though each has served me well when its service has been sorely needed.

No, the one after-dinner drink that for me can, at its best, turn a disastrous meal into, if not a triumph, at any rate a merely mild disappointment; the drink without which even a dinner composed of the most splendid dishes, accompanied by the noblest wines, remains oddly incomplete, like a beautifully-gowned woman in her stocking feet; is brandy.

And of all brandies, cognac.

For although cognac is brandy, not all brandy, as will be seen, is cognac. I have drunk much brandy in many places, for any country that grows wine can make brandy, and they all do—I think without exception. I have drunk local brandies, ranging from very good to perfectly disgusting, in Greece and Italy, in South Africa and Argentina, in Israel and Germany and Spain; I have been plied with what I was told was an old Portuguese brandy that might well have been made out of old Portuguese. And I must not forget—nay, I never shall forget—Naishapur, on the Golden Road to Samarkand, whither I travelled to visit the tomb of Omar Khayyam, and where I drank deep of Iranian

Grande Champagne Cognac Impériale, which is made by a company called Ararat, and smells of those chocolate creams that have crystallized violets on top.

I recall, too, that although in two years in Moscow in the early nineteen-fifties I could never lay lips, hard though I tried, on a decent glass of brandy, yet in 1959 in Kiev, where I found myself in the press party that accompanied Mr Macmillan and Mr Selwyn Lloyd on their official visit to the Soviet Union, there was served to us at our hotel a magnificent old brandy from Soviet Georgia, on which I got so fuddled through a long evening's session as to swear eternal friendship with Randolph Churchill.

Not that there was anything wrong with Randolph's friendship, but I was not in his class as a drinking man, and the prospect of an eternity of brandy sessions with Randolph stretching before me, from Kiev to East Bergholt, must have contributed as much as the fumes of alcohol to the hangover that accompanied me through the Ukraine for the next couple of days like a small, personal, black thundercloud, made to measure.

But although I will drink brandy anywhere, if not on the Randolphian scale, and would rather drink bad brandy than no brandy at all, my taste is not yet so depraved that I do not prefer good brandy to bad, and of all the good brandies I have drunk, whether to crown a meal or to drown my sorrows, the best have been from among the cognacs.

When Dr Johnson said that 'he who aspires to be a hero must drink brandy', it was tipsiness he was talking about, not taste, for he continued his tribute with, 'brandy will do soonest for a man what drinking *can* do for him' (Boswell's italics). (The reason that claret was only for boys was that 'a *man*'—my italics—'would be drowned by it before it made him drunk'.) That brandy will do it soonest is perhaps not quite so true now, when we can call upon 98-degree Russian and 140-degree-proof Polish vodkas, as Dr Johnson could not, but what is still truer of brandy than of vodka, and more true of cognac than of most brandies, is the doctor's further observation, that 'the flavour of brandy is most grateful to the palate'.

To mine, as to Dr Johnson's; and I owe a book to the liquor

that has provided not only mild anaesthesia, so that I have slept well in times of troubled mind and wretched memories, but what I suppose is a sort of aesthetic pleasure, when a bottle of good claret at one's own table or that of a like-minded friend has been followed by a glass far more strong, yet no less subtle. For there are depths and shallows, highlights and shades, of savour and of fragrance in a glass of cognac that for me no other distilled drink can offer. I am grateful to the good creature; hence this book.

Once I had decided that I should write a book on cognac, the question was: which cognac? For in previous books I had written about the champagne of one house, the claret of one house.

This time, any such choice was too difficult. I had been royally entertained in the past both by the Martells and the Hennessys, in Paris and in Cognac, and had drunk fine old brandies at their hospitable boards.

The partners in Denis-Mounié were old friends of mine; so were their brandies; and a tappit-hen of their admirable Réserve Edouard Sept had been presented to my son at his birth.

I thought highly of Hine—as who does not?—and had long ago discovered that Delamain Pale and Dry was particularly to my taste.

So, too, were—and are—the early-landed, late-bottled brandies that the French think the English a little dotty for doting upon: cognacs shipped here young and matured in wood under the sodden English skies, losing strength but gaining softness before being bottled. And I had enjoyed early-landed Exshaws, bought from Harveys of Bristol, Frapin from Stowells of Chelsea, Delamain from Corney and Barrow, Hine from Peter Dominic, old Augier and old Gautier. How could I single out one only of these names for a book without feeling that I had been churlish to all those other good friends?

That is how it comes about that this book is about cognac in general, not about any one cognac in particular. The decision meant that I had to decline kind offers from Martell, Hennessy and other houses to put me up during my last year's two visits (of three months in all) to Cognac, though I was able gratefully to accept the hotel bedroom put at my disposal by the Bureau National Interprofessionnel du Cognac, which represents the industry as a whole. It meant, too, rather more time-consuming trips than I had bargained for, because if one distinguished firm had been anxious to show me its distilleries and its vineyards, it would have been discourteous not to visit those of its closest rivals. If I interviewed one chief taster, it was morally obligatory to interview his opposite number.

Everyone was helpful, and I list my acknowledgments at the end of this introduction.

*　　*　　*

Before that, I have an explanation to make. In the following pages, I shall distinguish between the place and its product by using a capital initial for the one, Cognac, and lower-case for the other, cognac.

I made a similar statement, and followed the same principle, in my book *Bollinger*, only to be taken to task by my much respected colleague, Pamela Vandyke Price, in an otherwise flattering review in the *Spectator*, for what she termed the 'affected trend of not giving initial capital letters to wines such as Champagne, which are named after places'.

Were it not for that rap over the knuckles, I should not have thought that the practice needed defending. But Mrs Vandyke Price not only read English at my own university but is the acknowledged queen of my profession of writing about wine— wine correspondent of *The Times*, no less. What she says is, quite rightly, listened to.

So, lest her pronouncement has us all spattering our pages with parenthetical explanations—'Champagne (I mean the region)' and 'Champagne (I mean the wine)'—let me argue the stylistic case against her, as I would never presume to argue about a wine.

Hart's *Rules for Compositors and Readers at the University Press, Oxford* counsels 'lower-case initials for . . . objects named from persons and places', actually giving as an example 'un verre de champagne'. Collins's *Authors' and Printers' Dictionary* gives the same advice, and similar examples (' "champagne" a wine, as with "burgundy", but "Chambertin" a Burgundy wine'). And Rees's *Rules of Printed English* states firmly: 'In general avoid capitals wherever possible. A page clogged with capitals does not present a dignified appearance.'

Nor is there only appearance to consider: there is the logic of it. Would Mrs Vandyke Price really have one refer, perhaps in the same sentence, to claret and Burgundy; Champagne and sherry; hock and Moselle?

The complaint that a lower-case initial for champagne is an 'affected trend' suggests that it is new-fangled. Radical as my politics are, both my way of life and (I hope) my prose style are conservative, and far from my preferred usages being new-fangled, it is to be found in Lady Mary Wortley Montagu ('And we meet, with champagne and a chicken, at last') to Surtees, who referred to tops that had been cleaned with 'champagne and abricot jam'. I refrain from quoting such more recent writers as Rudyard Kipling and Bernard Shaw lest Mrs Vandyke Price regards them as being affectedly new-fangled.

Anyway, this is why I stick to the same usage, and why I wrote to Mrs Vandyke Price at the time to say that 'I am just back from Cognac, where I have begun work on a book about cognac'.

*   *   *

I must make another point about place-names. It will be clear from chapter 2 that throughout an interesting and significant period in the history of cognac, and until the end of the eighteenth century, the region from which it comes could only be accurately referred to as consisting largely of the provinces of Angoumois, Aunis and Saintonge. It was not until the Constitution of 1791 that these became the *départements* of Charente and Charente Inférieure. As it is more convenient to refer to the Charentes (and to the folk of the region as Charentais) than to keep on reciting the names of the three historic provinces, the reader will come across many a sentence in the following pages where I have sought readability rather than historical accuracy. I trust he will forgive me: it makes very little difference if he does not.

*   *   *

I feel more apologetic about what I recognize, more than any reviewer will, to be the inadequacies of this little book.

I did not set out to write a practical manual on how to produce cognac—merely an introductory sketch that would give my fellow brandy-lovers a rough but not inaccurate idea of what it is, how it is made and why, and what has been its history.

Even so, I am aware that the more technical aspects of vinification, distilling, ageing and blending have been treated very sketchily indeed. I have had to simplify to make matters understandable to my own mind, which is itself simple; I hope that the result is not too inadequate for subtler ones.

There are by-ways that I wish I had had more time to explore, with more space for an account of my explorations: the forests of Limousin and the Tronçais, for instance; why only their oak will do for cognac casks, and how those casks are made; Alfred de Vigny as a grower–distiller, and his correspondence with his bailiff; the historical relationship between French Protestantism and the cognac trade; the very future of that trade, which I am not alone in thinking may change both rapidly and radically.

I wish, in short, as many authors must wish, that I had had more time and more space, but chiefly that I had written a better book. My only excuse for offering what I feel myself to be inadequate is that, surprisingly, there is no one book in English, and never has been, devoted solely to the spirit that has delighted and consoled so many Englishmen for these three centuries. I hope that this, the first, will not be the last, but will offer some clues and some starting-points for livelier pens and more scholarly minds than mine.

*   *   *

I have already mentioned the room put at my disposal in Cognac by the Bureau National Interprofessionnel du Cognac.

I am additionally grateful to Monsieur Henri Coquillaud, Directeur of the Bureau, to his colleagues Colonel Gérard Sturm and Madame Nina Raffoux, and to Monsieur José Lacour, head of the bureau's Division de la Documentation et des Etudes Economiques et Fiscales, for much statistical and other information, for patience under questioning about the structure of the trade and its problems, and for effecting introductions and making appointments.

Then, though, as I have explained, I felt constrained to decline invitations to stay at any one of the hospitable houses of Cognac, I received great help in every other possible way, from the opening of ancient archives to the tapping of ancient casks, in virtually every house in the region that is at all notable for age, size or the particular distinction of its product. It would be invidious to list them in any other than alphabetical order, which I do here, with the names of those members of each firm with whom I made contact, many of whom were kindly hosts at luncheon or at dinner, as well as lucid mentors and preceptors in what for a couple of years, at home and abroad, has been my special subject. I dispense with the full titles of the various firms, and give the names by which they are best and most simply known:

Augier: Comte Jacques Burignot de Varenne
Bisquit-Dubouché: MM. D. N. Bona, Bernard Detré, J. d'Indy and Louis Renard
Camus: MM. Philippe Camus and Willem Grothe
Comandon: Monsieur Philippe Mitterrand
Courvoisier: Monsieur Christian Braastad and Mr John D. Powe
Delamain: MM. Noël Sauzey and Alain Braastad-Delamain
Denis-Mounié: MM. Richard and Jacques Roullet
Exshaw: Monsieur Henri Exshaw
Gautier Frères: MM. Gonzague Hériard Dubreuil and Michel Massemin
Hennessy: Comte Alain de Pracomtal and Monsieur Maurice Fillioux
Hine: MM. Robert and Bernard Hine
Martell: MM. Francis Arnaud, François Chapeau and Pierre Cordier, and Mr Nicholas M. Burnet
Otard: Monsieur Gérard de Ramefort
Prunier: Monsieur Claude Burnez
Rémy-Martin: MM. Patrick Quien and N. A. Schuman
Salignac: Monsieur Hervé de Jarnac

Union Coopérative de Viticulteurs Charentais
(Prince Hubert de Polignac brand): MM. Bernard Lucquiaud
and Erling Wolf

In addition, I had interesting and helpful conversations with
Monsieur Noël Dor and Monsieur Jean Fréderic Gautier-
Auriol of the small family firms of A. E. Dor and Guy Gautier
respectively; and I learned much from Monsieur Marcel Ragnaud, who makes a single-vineyard cognac on his own property
at Ambleville, and from Monsieur Gaston Raffoux, a *bouilleur
de cru*, besides being entertained most hospitably in the bosoms
of their respective families.

MM. Lucien Breton and Pierre Lecland showed me and explained the Breton fruits-in-cognac factory at Barbezieux;
Monsieur Maurice Braud told me about the cognac he buys for
that excellent liqueur Grand Marnier and explained how it is
used; Monsieur Gaston Courant did as much for the various
cognac-based liqueurs he makes in Cognac itself.

In my researches into cask-making I was helped by Monsieur
Jean Taransaud of the Tonnellerie Taransaud in Cognac, by
Monsieur Nicaud of Nicaud et Cie, Limoges, and by Monseiur
Camille Gagnon of Ygrande, Honorary President of the Amis de
Tronçais. Monsieur Gérard Mienné of the Compagnie de
Saint-Gobain was similarly helpful about glass and the manu-
facture of bottles.

Monsieur and Madame Jean-Marie Sallée of the Cognac
bureau of the newspaper *Sud-Ouest* helped to elucidate for me the
guerre du Cognac of 1971, and even found a place for me, though—
diplomatically—not a banner, in a peaceful demonstration outside the offices of the Bureau National so that I could help to
demand (I think) a reclassification of the vineyards of Blanzac,
to which I had hitherto been a stranger, from *fins bois* to *petite
champagne*.

In the matter of the *-ac* endings to the region's place-names I
sought (and found) help from Mr Hal Milner-Gulland, head-
master of Cumnor House School, Danehill, Sussex, and his
friend Monsieur Jean-Louis Galet of Perigueux; from Dr Glyn
Daniel of Cambridge and, through him, from Professor Kenneth

Jackson, of the Department of Celtic Languages, Literatures, History and Antiquities at Edinburgh.

On the same, and similar, subjects I learned much from Monsieur Alain Braastad-Delamain, whose help in his capacity as a blender of cognac I have already acknowledged, but who was also a scholarly guide to the history and architecture of the region and to the customs and language of its people.

His wife, and Comtesse Alain de Pracomtal, Mesdames Hervé de Jarnac, Marcel Ragnaud, Gaston Raffoux and Maurice Braud, whose husbands I have already mentioned, were kind enough to entertain me in their homes, as were Monsieur and Madame Peytoureau, with their friend Miss Diana Dickson.

Mr Michael Broadbent of Christie's kindly made the drawings of brandy glasses reproduced on page 135, and was enlightening (and amusing) about 'Napoleon' brandies. Mr George Ordish generously allowed me to read, before publication, and to quote from, proofs of his important work on the phylloxera, *The Great Wine Blight*; and I am indebted to Mr Brian Roberts, author of *Ladies in the Veld*, for the note on p. 119 about the references to Courvoisier in the Natal newspapers of 1880. Evelyn Waugh's *Brideshead Revisited* is quoted on page 133 by kind permission of A. D. Peters & Co, and the quotation from Charles Morgan's *The Voyage* on page 22 is by kind permission of Macmillan of London and Basingstoke.

Such parts of my book as deal with the past—with the history of the region, of the trade, and of the art of distilling—are based upon published material: the more important of the books I have consulted are referred to in a bibliographical note. Reference to Robert Delamain's *Histoire du Cognac* was made all the easier for me by Lieut.-Col. Andrew Graham, who kindly lent me the manuscript translation he made in the long months during which he was lost to his many friends in a nursing-home.

My secretary, Miss Jennifer Higgie, has deciphered my cramped handwriting with what must sometimes have been inspired guesswork, and I am most grateful to her and to my wife for the skill and enthusiasm they brought to the compilation of an index.

For two or three weeks of my second spell in Cognac I was

joined by my old friend Reginald Peck, uninhibitedly cele-
brating—as who would not?—his then impending retirement
from the *Daily Telegraph* bureau in Bonn. But for him, I should
have got through more work and less cognac.

Finally, I am also, I suppose, indebted to the Syndicat d'In-
itiative of Cognac, to which I formally presented myself on each
of the visits I paid while working on this book. The first time,
they gave me a plan of the town; the second time, some picture
postcards advertising Hennessy.

1. The Heart of the Matter

T HE *Oxford English Dictionary* devotes three and a half of its three-column pages to the substantive 'Spirit'. The twenty-first of its twenty-four major definitions is, 'a liquid of the nature of an essence or extract from some substance, esp. one obtained by distillation. . . .'

Cognac is such a spirit.

Other definitions in the same dictionary call upon such evocative words and phrases as, 'the animating or vital principle', 'life-blood' and 'soul'.

Cognac is such a spirit, too—the soul or vital principle of the wine it is distilled from. It is, as it were, the heart of the matter, arrived at by the process of distillation.

The word 'distillation' derives from the Latin *destillare*, a verb found in Virgil, in Pliny and in Seneca (though not in Cicero) and known to the translators of the Vulgate, as meaning to drop or to trickle down.

It is an entirely appropriate derivation, for distillation is the process of turning a liquid into vapour by heating it, and then recovering it in liquid form by condensation. The simplest and most familiar example of distillation, because the rain it raineth every day, is the vapourizing of surface water into clouds by the heat of the sun, and the subsequent condensation of the resultant vapour, by cooling, into rain—how right the Romans were!—that drops or trickles down.

A simple extension of the process is based upon the fact that different liquids boil and, as a result, become vapour at different temperatures. By heating a mixed liquid, the more volatile components will be given off first, and can be condensed and collected as the 'heart' or 'soul'—the quintessence—of the original mixture, leaving the rest behind.

In wine there is both alcohol and water, along with other, minor, constituents. Alcohol boils and becomes vapour at 78·3 degrees Centigrade (173 degrees Fahrenheit), water at a hundred: thus, the alcohol in wine can be separated by distillation from the water and other, similar, substances.

The process was known to the ancients. Pliny's use, to which I have already referred, of the verb *destillare* occurs in his account of the extraction, by boiling, of spirits of turpentine from resin, and a Greek writer of the fifth century A.D. wrote of the distillation of a sort of universal cure, or panacea, from a boiling mixture of sulphur, lime and water. None of these, and other, classical references to distillation, though, concern the extraction of alcohol from wine.

At one time, virtually all the authorities held that although wine is known to have been made by the fermentation of grape-juice in Neolithic times, some ten to twelve thousand years ago, the distillation from it of an alcoholic spirit had to wait until the alembic was devised by the Arabs, whose secret reached the Western world by way of the Moors in Spain.

In support of this opinion, two thirteenth-century Spaniards, Ramon Lull and Arnaldus de Villa Nova, are quoted. Lull, the mystic, was long regarded as the author of a *Testamentum* in which occurs a recipe for the extraction of brandy from 'the blackest of black wine'. It is now thought that the work is apocryphal, but what is considered significant is that, whoever the author, he must have been, as Lull is known to have been, a student of Arabic and of alchemy and, also like Lull, resident in Spain during the Moorish occupation.

Arnaldus de Villa Nova was another Spaniard of the time to whom have been attributed recipes for or references to the distillation of brandy from wine. Again, the quoted works may or may not be apocryphal; again, the place and the period are held to be none the less significant.

It seems to have been only recently that these claims on behalf of the Arabs and the Moors of Spain have been challenged.

The erudite William Younger, whose *Gods, Men and Wine* was published in 1966, after his early death, considered it 'extremely doubtful that the Arabs knew about alcohol and more than probable that it [the distillation of alcohol from wine] was discovered by twelfth-century Christians at Salerno'.

The equally scholarly Edward Hyams, also writing in the nineteen-sixties, is not so doubtful as Younger was about the Arabs' acquaintance—despite the teachings of the Prophet—with alcohol. He is prepared to admit the possibility of their having been the first, or among the first, to use the distilling techniques already known in the ancient world and, nearer to their own time, by Nestorian Christian alchemists; to improve the apparatus and the technique; and to extract spirit from wine.

He claims, though, to have found 'a small amount of evidence' that the Chinese (who also may have learned about distilling from the Nestorians, either directly or through the Turkish peoples who had settled and were growing wine in Iran) were distilling spirit from wine rather earlier than any of the peoples of the West. He points out, too, that for that matter, although no one has claimed the distinction for the alchemists of the Eastern Roman Empire, they did have stills in their laboratories: they might have been inquisitive enough to see what happened if one put wine into them. Or they might not.

As for our use of the Arabic words 'alcohol' and 'alembic', he dismisses the notion that this is proof that the Arabs invented the art of producing the one by means of the other: it is true, he says, that the Europeans who took up alchemy received it at the hands of Arab masters, but what they took from Moorish books, using the Arabic words they found therein for phenomena which had no names in European tongues, the Moorish authors had themselves taken from Alexandrian authors.

* * *

However all this may be, there is no doubt that by the thirteenth century the technique of distilling spirit from wine was widely known and widely practised.

It is a commonplace to historians of ideas and of techniques that at any one time there will be men of an enquiring turn of mind, widely separated from each other in space, in language, in culture and in technical resources, working unknown to each other on the same problems. When mankind is ready for wireless telegraphy, for the internal combustion engine, for the zip fastener or for the atom bomb, it is always on the point of being invented, in France and Germany, Italy and the United States, all at the same time. And it may well be that some Andorran or Nicaraguan of fertile mind has also got the principles of the same thing down on paper, but lacks the technical resources to get it off the drawing-board and into production.

(In Stalin's time, we used to ridicule claims that Russian scientists had invented, as it might be, the sewing-machine or the aeroplane. The claims were made by propagandists of the régime, primarily for internal consumption, in an attempt to dispel the inferiority that Soviet citizens were thought to feel in face of the technical achievements of the West. When, as a newspaper correspondent in Moscow in the early nineteen-fifties, I set about enquiring into some of these claims, sure enough there was always a set of faded drawings or portfolio of detailed manuscript notes in this or that library or museum to prove that some Russian had indeed been working on the particular problem at the appropriate time. The West had always got in first simply because Tsarist Russia lacked the resources of nineteenth-century or early twentieth-century Britain or Germany or United States. But the idea had been in men's minds all over the world at about the same time.)

So it was that the thirteenth century found spirits being distilled from wine in Spain, in Italy, and in China—where it seems to have been achieved by freezing rather than by boiling (as applejack has been made in Canada, and eau-de-vie in Calvados) and where some believed that the resultant 'spirit and fluid secretion of wine', if imbibed, 'will penetrate into a man's armpits and he will die'.

That spirits could be distilled from grain was an earlier discovery, and there seems to be no connection between the one and the other: in this instance, for all that I have said about the universality of ideas, there seems to have been a thought barrier between the Irish and Scottish and German distillers of primitive sorts of schnapps and whisky on the one hand and, on the other, the Chinese and Byzantine and Spanish distillers of brandy of a sort.

Never mind whether St Patrick, as some pious folk believe, not only drove the snakes from Ireland but taught its saints and scholars to make potheen: it is certain, at any rate, that when Henry II invaded the country in 1172 he found the distillation of whiskey from grain well established: Professor David Daiches quotes a Scottish scholar–poet who maintained that the Irish invented and used it as an embrocation for their sick mules, and that only the Scots would ever have thought of drinking it.

It is curious that the French, by no means the least quick-witted of peoples, should have lagged behind their Iberian neighbours to the south and their Hibernian neighbours to the north in the production of ardent spirits. But I know of no evidence to show that any sort of spirit was being distilled in France, whether from grain, grape, or other fruit, before the fourteenth century. It may be that they were happy enough with their wines, already of outstandingly high quality compared with those of other countries, until the Italians, from whom they learned much in the way of good living, taught them to drink, to enjoy and, in consequence, to make distilled and flavoured liqueurs.

But if they were slow to begin, the French learned quickly enough and well enough to outstrip their masters, and to distil spirits too benign to fly to a man's armpits and kill him, too subtle to squander upon sick mules. Some of the greatest liqueurs, *eaux de vie des fruits* and brandies now come from France; this is the story of the greatest of them all.

2. The Place

HALF-WAY along the five hundred miles or so of France's Atlantic coast, at Rochefort, on latitude 46 degrees north, immediately south of La Rochelle, is the mouth of the river Charente. Rising in the relatively high country between Limoges and Angoulême, the river slows down as it leaves the latter city for lower ground, and meanders lazily westwards through the seventy or eighty miles of richly fertile pasture and arable, woodland and vineyard, that lie between the edge of the Limousin plateau and the ocean.

It winds gently through what were once the provinces of Angoumois, Aunis and Saintonge,[1] which since the Revolution have been the *départements* of the two Charentes—Charente and

[1] Though a small part of what was once Angoumois is now in the *département* Haute-Vienne.

Charente Maritime[2]—a cosy countryside referred to generally as Les Charentes, or the Charentais.

At its very heart, on the river itself, and almost straddling the border between the two Charentes, lies the small grey town of Cognac, which gives its name to the world's most famous brandy (and the name of which is taken, without permission, for some of the most infamous).

French law limits that name (and the law of many other civilized countries follows that of France) to the strictly controlled distilled wine of this region, a region that includes the whole of the Charente Maritime and all that part (rather more than two-thirds) of the Charente that lies west of a line from Ruffec to La Rochefoucauld. It corresponds exactly to the eighteenth-century Generalité de La Rochelle—pre-Revolutionary administrative divisions were based upon natural boundaries —and covers some 4,300 square miles.

As we shall see, though, by no means every part of this region produces cognac, although it is entitled to, and those parts that do produce it do not all produce cognac of the same quality. About fifty per cent of the whole area is cultivable, but only some twelve and a half per cent of this cultivable area is at present growing grapes for cognac. The vineyards are not, of course, spread evenly over the region: in the most favoured parts, as much as sixty-three per cent of the cultivable area is growing grapes for cognac: in the least-favoured a mere three per cent.

*   *   *

It is hard to believe, as one drives through this bland, temperate, unexotic countryside, that the town of Cognac is on the same latitude as the southernmost tip of Lake Maggiore and rather to the south of Como; on the same latitude as Trieste and rather to the south of Zagreb.

[2] Until 1940, the *département* that is now Charente Maritime was Charente Inférieure—meaning simply 'lower' or 'downstream' Charente. But just as the people of what until the Second World War was Bas Médoc appealed successfully to have the 'Bas' deleted, so the Saintongeois argued against the seemingly derogatory implication of 'Inférieure', and won their case.

For here there are no snow-capped mountains to terminate the prospect, no blaze of bougainvillea under a southern sun; here no lemon-trees bloom. Nor are there the deep snows and bitter winds of a Balkan winter, the gritty heat of a Balkan summer.

This is an Atlantic, not a Mediterranean or an Alpine, not an Adriatic or a Balkan 46 degrees north: an arm of the Gulf Stream makes mild the Charentais winter—snow is infrequent in Cognac, and mimosa blooms in February on the Isle of Oléron—while the breezes of the western ocean temper the warmth of summer.

In writing a few years ago of the Médoc[3] I quoted Cyril Connolly's observation that its climate is 'as near perfection as a temperate maritime climate can be . . . it is southern England removed to the furthest point at which it would remain both green and industrious'.

What is true of the Médoc is pretty well as true of the region around Cognac, which is seventy miles north of Bordeaux and although further from the sea is not protected against it, as the Médoc is, by the high dunes and the thick pine-forests of the Landes.

All, or almost all, that there is here that speaks of the south is Cognac's fame as a rugby-footballing town. In this respect, this is where the Sud-Ouest begins, for Cognac is the northernmost outpost of the stamping-ground of the greatest French teams and footballers, who play the game (if that is the appropriate phrase) with Gascon vehemence. Its own team is made up of tigers lured from Lourdes, or poached from Pau, with the offers of jobs humping casks or, if they can read and write, in the counting-houses of Martell or of Hennessy.

That, and the other forms of wild life that whisper occasionally of the south; for, although it is cool here of an autumn evening, there are screens on the windows against local *moustiques* that are as dashing as d'Artagnan's *mousquetaires* (though d'Artagnan himself came from farther south still, from Armagnac, where the other great brandy is made).

[3] Cyril Ray, *Lafite: The Story of Chateau Lâfite-Rothschild*, London and New York, 1968.

And the tiled roofs, blackened by brandy-fumes, have the shallow pitch of the south.

*　　*　　*

France is two-and-a-half times the size of the island of Britain, and has a slightly smaller population: as Patrick Brogan has pointed out, in *The Times*, 'you can drive for miles without seeing a village, and you can drive for hundreds of miles without meeting a town larger than Brighton'. The Charentes is a particularly rich, well-farmed and, by French standards, thickly-populated agricultural region, but in the ninety miles from Angoulême, which is less than a third the size of Brighton, to La Rochelle, which is half the size, the three towns of Cognac, Saintes, and Rochefort,[4] quite the biggest of the other towns in the area, are each about as big as Lichfield, Winchester and Clacton respectively.

Villages are fewer, farther between, and smaller than they would be in a similar English countryside (less lavishly supplied, too, with the amenities and technical resources of modern life: I have it from the mayor himself, Max Cointreau, that there was no telephone in the *Mairie* of the sizeable village of Gensac, near Cognac, until 1968). In the biggest of them there might be a cinema with showings on two evenings a week, one village television set in the one village café, and a restaurant that clearly does not expect tourists, for it does not set out on the pavement one of those come-hither cut-out figures that beckon the motorist on more frequented routes; but that offers an uncommonly good *prix fixe* luncheon to a few local regulars and to the occasional commercial traveller, who will have breakfasted at Angoulême and will dine and sleep at La Rochelle. So there are no rooms at the inn.

As often as not, the big houses of well-to-do growers are not in the villages themselves, but on the outskirts, or tucked away down rutted lanes between one village and the next.

They are vast but secretive, the great, heavy double gates that open on to the lane or street being set into high blank walls behind which the farm and domestic buildings stand about a

---

[4] Populations approximately 22,500, 28,000 and 34,800 respectively.

partly grassed, partly cobbled, courtyard. Their ancestry is clearly Roman, as William Younger pointed out, but at one remove, by way of the Romanesque churches of the region, for they were not built before the first decades or so of the seventeenth century, when the Dutch shippers and traders brought quick and big money to the Charentais (see chapter 3).

The first page of Charles Morgan's *The Voyage* gives a good idea, though the Hazard house had been altered just before the story opens. (Charles Morgan lived in Jarnac with members of the Delamain family, who blend a noble cognac, while he was writing his novel, just before the war):

'The house, an old one, had been given by its extensions the shape of an L which included, within its arms, a courtyard facing south and east over the valley of the Charente. Formerly this courtyard had been shut in by the high walls usual in that secretive countryside, but when Julien Hazard died in 1876, his son . . . had pulled down the walls to what he called 'sitting-level' and for the last seven years had enjoyed an outlook denied to his childhood. The great stone gateway at the south-east corner remained; for a stone gateway with rounded arch, perhaps suggested long ago by the Romanesque façades of the local churches, was the pride of a Charentais home. . . .

'At the back of the L were two walled courtyards. The larger, to the west, had at its farther end, facing the house, the customary gateway, and, on either side, the farm buildings, the stables, the store-houses and the distillery in which the business of vine-grower and farmer was carried on.'

A motorist on a main road at the very edge of the town of Cognac itself, which is at the centre of the district, can be held up by a waddling line of geese or, as dusk falls, by a herd of black-and-white Friesians ambling sedately from meadow to byre, with a woman on a bicycle in the van and another at their rear, each bearing a red flag.

For, measured by area, if not by value, this is as much vegetable-growing, sheep-raising and dairy-farming as it is wine-growing country. The Charente floods in winter-time and, while there are sheep on the modest slopes above the flooding area, the cows grazing in the lush green water-meadows give a butter richer and finer even—more expensive, too, in the smart food-shops around the Madeleine in Paris—than almost all if not all those of Normandy. This is a region rich in milk, butter, cream and wine, as Curnonsky, '*le prince élu des gastronomes*', pointed out: '*la base sacrée de toute cuisine digne de ce nom*'.[5]

(It is interesting that, unlike Normandy, this is not particularly good cheese country. The Charentais say that the Normans make their best milk and cream into cheese, which is why the Norman butter is not so good as theirs: *they* make the best butter by putting their best milk and cream into it—you can always buy cheese from somewhere else.

Note, too, that Curnonsky makes no mention of melons. I have eaten many a *charentais* melon in the Charentes: I think they all came from the Var, in the south, and that *charentais* is applied to a melon now to indicate type, merely, though no doubt it once signified provenance as well.)

*   *   *

In the most favourable and favoured areas for the grape, around Cognac itself, there are some few stretches on either side of the road where there is nothing in view save the rows of vines, but mostly the vineyards are to be seen scattered among meadows where the cattle are meditatively munching, and the curves of meadows and lines of vineyards are themselves broken by clumps of trees. Except by the river itself, it is gently undulating country, with neither the great sweeps of downland one sees in Champagne nor the long, flat vistas of the Médoc, and without either region's great unbroken stretches of vines. And not only in the long summer days but, it has seemed to me, in spring and winter too, even when it floods the meadows, the Charente seems hardly to flow, to be more lake than river, reflecting as sharply as a picture-postcard grey walls, and willows that are almost always green.

A. E. Housman once wrote of Oxfordshire that its great

[5] Curnonsky and Marcel Rouff, *La France Gastronomique: (L'Aunis, La Saintonge, L'Angoumois)*, Paris, 1924.

claim 'is the wide horizon you command even from a slight elevation'. In the Cognac country all the elevations—even, at its edge, the ramparts of Angoulême, on its bluff above the river—are slight indeed, yet the horizons here, too, are wide. Perhaps it is this wideness of horizon, perhaps the relative nearness of the sea—for one is reminded of the Channel coast, the Côte d'Opale, and of the men who painted its skies—that except in the most inclement weather gives a nacreous quality to the light here, a gentle luminosity, that every visitor remarks upon, and every native boasts about.

Jacques de Lacretelle, who discounts the effects of the sea—he writes that the light of the region is neither that of the Midi nor that of the Atlantic coast—uses the word '*tamisée*', filtered.

Pierre Loti, born in Rochefort, remembered under the blaze of Far-Eastern skies, and by the seas that beat upon Icelandic shores, the soft light and the cool woodlands of the Charentes, and sang them in that essay on the Sleeping Beauty that led authority to save from decay the Château de la Roche Courbon, on the edge of the cognac country. And Eugène Fromentin, though he left the Charentes for Algeria to paint his salon pictures, set his sad, romantic novel *Dominique* among the vineyards he had known as a boy—'pensive and peaceful and warm, life here must be very tranquil'—catching with a painter's eye the soft radiance of summer moonlight, the grave charm of autumn, 'our singularly mild climate that made winter bearable', and 'April's bath of light'.

Always, it is the light. . . .

Louis Ravaz, first head of the Viticultural Research Station of Cognac, wrote in his *Le Pays de Cognac* in 1900 that the Charentes was noted for its '*climat doux, aux moeurs douces*'.

Louis Larmet dedicated volume VI, the Cognac volume, of his classic *Atlas de la France Vinicole*, 'Devotedly to my native city of Saintes, *en cette douce et lumineuse Saintonge . . .*', just as twenty years earlier Curnonsky, in his gastronomic survey of the region, already quoted, had written, '*douce, bien douce*'; it is all in clean, clear lines; in peaceful, harmonious horizons; in little copses, beautiful parkland, gently rolling country, cool and shady woodland . . . and all this landscape, the charm of which slowly lulls you, takes possession of you, speaking of the happiness of a country life, is bathed in a sunshine that never burns or dazzles, under a soft, pearly sky'.

Jacques Chardonne, too, recalling in 1938 his boyhood in Barbezieux, remembered that 'the light of the Charente is quite peculiar to this region, and to none other. Only a little further away, you find a different sky, a different way of life. I never knew, even in my childhood, summers such as burned in the pages of François Mauriac, although we and his Médoc were near neighbours. *La Charente est plus douce.*'[6]

All four of them—the viticulturist, the cartographer, the gastronome, the essayist—use the word '*douce*'.

This is not the place to write about the region's Roman remains and Romanesque churches, or about Angoulême, Saintes and La Rochelle, interesting though each city is, historically and architecturally. No one spending any time in the region should miss them; Freda White is an admirable guide.[7]

But they are border-towns, as it were, of the cognac country— just in it, but not in any real sense of it. (It is true that one small, old-established brandy house has its headquarters in Saintes, but there is also one, for that matter, in Bordeaux.)

Nor must I let my pen linger here—not at any rate for too long—as in the past I have happily let myself linger, on the islands of Ré and Oléron, where I have drunk the thin local wine, which would have been cognac if it could, and eaten the delicious local asparagus. Not even in the little township of Marennes, on the mainland opposite Oléron, straggling across and around its creeks and marshes and oyster-beds, where I have stuffed myself with shellfish raw, shellfish cooked, shellfish hot, shellfish cold, and shellfish soups of pretty nearly every kind for pretty nearly next to nothing, and whence its delicacies are delivered daily by road, along with those of La Rochelle, through Rochefort, all over the Charentes.

Curnonsky could have added fish and shellfish to his list of milk and butter, cream and wine, as the culinary blessings of this

---

[6] Jacques Chardonne, *Le Bonheur de Barbezieux*, Paris, 1938.
[7] Freda White, *Ways of Aquitaine*, London, 1968.

happy region, for there are always mussels on every Cognac menu, or *mouclade*, which is a cream-and-mussel stew, or *la chaudrée*, which is a mixed-fish stew, a sort of *bouillabaisse*, and in little village restaurants farther inland even than Cognac, perhaps fifty miles from the sea, yet served regularly from Marennes, you will often be given four or six oysters with your mixed hors d'oeuvre of *crudités* as part of a four-course, twelve-franc meal. (I have seen a child of about five or six, lunching in La Rochelle with his parents, get through his dozen as part of a sixteen-franc meal: they were served in the French way, so that his mother had to sever each one from its shell for him.)

All of which is to say nothing of the local snails, which are called *cagouilles* throughout the region except around La Rochelle, in what used to be the province of Aunis, where they are *lumas*.

At the very end of 1971, when letters to editors and feature articles in the Beaverbrook press were all insisting that entry into the Common Market would mean dearer food for the hapless English housewife and diner-out, I was served this *repas* at the only restaurant in Gondeville, seven or eight miles east of Cognac—the village itself, let alone its restaurant, too small to be in the Guide Michelin:

> six oysters with unlimited bread and Charentais butter,
> a dish of mixed *crudités*,
> a lemon sole, *meuniére* in Charentais butter,
> three thick slices of roast pork with fried potatoes and a
>   green salad,
> cheese, and
> a choice of fruit—I had a huge pear.

I had arrived unannounced; there was no menu; I was given the meal of the day, as offered to everyone; I helped myself to red and white wine; and was charged eleven francs—service, tax, and wine included.

There were thirteen francs to the pound at the time and eleven francs were worth about $2.

Fairly typical, perhaps a bit better than some, where you might be given only four oysters, and charged as much as twelve francs.

One of the commonest local eating customs in these parts, from the coast to Angoulême, is to serve oysters on the shell along with tiny hot garlic sausages, which you eat one each to a mouthful, hot and cold alternately, the combination of fish and meat a sort of symbolic marriage of the region's riches from land and from sea. An agreeable alternative, offered at the Restaurant du Centre at Jarnac as *huîtres à la charentaise*, is oysters served with pheasant pâté, bread and butter.

Much as these oyster-beds contribute, though, to the gastronomic pleasures of the region, and although the border-cities of Angoulême and Saintes and La Rochelle handsomely ornament it, they play no part in producing the region's greatest glory. The cognac towns are Jarnac and Segonzac, Barbezieux, Jonzac and, of course, Cognac itself.

Four out of the five names I mention, it will be noticed, end in -ac, which is a pretty fair average for the district, where -ac endings are commoner even than -den and -hurst in the Weald of Kent, or -by and -thorpe in Lincolnshire.

There are those who should know better who hold that the -ac ending is short for *aqua*, water—that just as this whole south-western region of France was Aquitania to the Romans, Aquitaine to the French (Guienne is a corruption of it), because it was a place of waters, so in the same way every town or village with an -ac ending to its name was at a spring or a source or a well.

Nothing of the sort: the Latin *aqua* becomes -aix, -ax or -évian in southern French place-names, -eau in the north.

Nor is it quite true, though it is much more nearly so, to say as Philip Oyler did in *The Generous Earth* that the place-names with -ac endings 'indicate their Roman origin and long occupation, for the ending -ac is simply an abbreviated form of -acum, the Latin genitive plural'.

It is not. It is an abbreviation of the Gaulish adjectival suffixes *-acos* (masculine), *-aca* (feminine), or *-acon* (neuter), which in most cases become -é or -y in northern French, -ac, -at or -as in southern, meaning the estate or the manor or the domain of a person (or the place of a natural feature). In Britain, the Romano-British town-name Eburacum, whence come both Ebor and York, meant

27

probably 'the estate of Eburos'—Eburos being a British, not a Roman, name. Cognac was the estate of Comnius.

Place-names and other words in these parts derive in the southern way from Latin, not the northern: the endings become -ac, not -é or -y. In spite of the fact that one does not feel here, as one does to some extent in Bordeaux, completely in Bayonne, that this is in any sense the south of France, it is nevertheless the Languedoc, the country of the *langue d'oc* where the word for 'yes' was '*oc*' and not that of the *langue d'oil*, in the centre and the north, where the word was '*oil*' and has become '*oui*'.

Freda White explains it clearly in *Ways of Aquitaine*: when the Roman legions marched away, leaving France to the indigenous Gauls and the incoming Visigoths and Franks, the Teutons of the east went on using Germanic dialects, but those to the west took to 'the demotic Latin that had become the language of camp and market over the centuries'. South of the Loire, where the Gauls had long been familiar with soldiers' Latin, and had made it their own, this developed into the *langue d'oc*, an easy, relaxed, Romance tongue; to the north, the Franks were thicker on the ground and took to demotic Latin as a foreign language, using it more formally and grammatically as the *langue d'oil*.

To this day, says Miss White, the people of the south-west are apt to say of themselves that they are Gallo-Romans. And I have been told by Claude Burnez of the Cognac house of Prunier, himself a most distinguished archaeologist, how easily at digs near Cognac the local peasants and visiting youngsters from Montpellier understood each others' dialect—the locals would have found it harder to understand much nearer neighbours from the north. (The region of the -ac endings extends from not very far north of Cognac just about to Montpellier. Those outlying -ac endings that one finds in Brittany are attributed by Monsieur Burnez to seaborne traffic, dating almost from prehistoric times, between Breton ports of La Rochelle and Rochefort.)

*　　*　　*

Of those towns and villages that I have mentioned with their

-ac endings, Cognac, they say, is the world's best-known French place-name after that of Paris itself.

Ardouin-Dumazet's story[8] has been often quoted (and at least as often misquoted):

'It was at a council in Rome that Monsignor Cousseau,[9] bishop of Angoulême, was exchanging civilities in Latin with the bishops who had come from every corner of the realm—prelates-cum-conquistadores from North [sic] America, big-wigs who were half Peruvian-Indian, bishops from Ireland. Each introduced himself with the name of his bishopric. For most of the bishops, these diocesan titles conveyed nothing. This was especially true of the Venezuelan princes of the church, to whom "Bishop of Engolisma, in the Charente" was meaningless: their blank looks made this obvious.

Monsignor Cousseau had an idea worthy of a genius: "Which means", he said, "that I am Bishop of Cognac".

And everybody there—bishops, archbishops, cardinals—all cried out with an air of envy and admiration:

"Cognac! Cognac! What a splendid bishopric!" '

All the same, however world-renowned its name, Cognac is a dull place. It seems sometimes almost as if it is muffled by the curious velvety black, soot-like deposit that darkens its walls and roofs—a fungus that thrives on the fumes that escape by evaporation from the town's millions of brandy-casks. (This fungus was identified in 1881 by Dr Richon as the *torula de Cognac*, now the *Torula Compinacensis Richon*.)

It is a little smaller than the champagne town of Epernay and, like Epernay, its shops—less elegant than Epernay's—and its indifferent cafés and restaurants are disposed about the central square, where François Premier, who was born here, prances perpetually in bronze, and around which far more heavy traffic clanks and rumbles its way than is agreeable, holding up more light traffic than one expects to come across in so small a town.

Not much of a tourist-centre itself, Cognac is visited briefly in the summer by tourists on the wing between Switzerland and

[8] In his *Voyage en France, les Charentes*, 1898.
[9] Antoine-Charles Cousseau, 1805-75; bishop of Angoulême, 1850-72.

the Atlantic coast, between Paris or the conurbations of the north-east and the Pyrenees. There are other people here all the year round, bent on business in brandy. Its own world-famous product is delivered now by road, as once it was largely by river and canal, to the Atlantic and the Channel and the Mediterranean ports, and by road, too, to Paris and the other great cities of France. So are the dairy products of the region. Through the streets of Cognac, too, and round the statue of François Premier, come fish and shellfish from Marennes and La Rochelle, and back by road go whatever could be worth the people of the coast swapping their oysters for. Out by road goes glass from the huge Saint Gobain factory on the edge of the town, and in from Limoges and the forest of Tronçais comes timber for the coopers of Cognac.

The streets are all the more congested because Cognac is ill-served by the railway. As it is on a modest branch line appro-priate to its size but not to its importance, the people of Cognac and its visitors must change at Saintes for Bordeaux, and at Angoulême for Paris and for virtually everywhere else.

This is the true measure of the town, as it was the true measure of Bonn, not all that many years ago, when it was the only European capital at which the trains did not stop.

Were it not, indeed, for those *camions* thundering ceaselessly round the Place François-Premier; were it not for the youngsters arriving on their mopeds of an evening to shout down the television sets in the cafés; were it not for the even more re-sounding fame of its product, Cognac would still be what one would call a sleepy little country town. 'Sleepy' in a spiritual sense, at any rate.

In the sense, that is, that for most of the three months that I lived there in the winter of 1971 the clock on the Palais de Justice stood always at eleven. The stamp-machine at the central post office was always out of order, and so always was one of the swing-doors. The town museum, which has little more than a few token exhibits to illustrate a world-famous industry and product, is open on four half-days a week, and the municipal library, even less rewarding to the earnest student of cognac, only on three.

The Place

When the 700 or so employees at Martell's main establishment in the very middle of the town go off on their bicycles and in their motor-cars for their two-hour luncheon break—no nonsense here about staff canteens or packets of sandwiches—nobody turns a key in a lock, no watchman goes on duty. Who in their own home-town, seems to be the attitude, would pinch a handbag, a bottle of the best—or a cask of 1895 cognac?

And I have no reason to suppose that Hennessy, round the corner, or any other of the great houses, is any less trusting. This is small-town provincial France.

The only touch of style or of swagger in the whole place is the peacock that struts the lawns in the charming little park surrounding the Hôtel de Ville, seeming to sneer, as well a peacock might, at the inscription over the portico: 'Liberté, Egalité, Fraternité'.

For in this region the traffic and the youngsters on their mopeds and the television-sets in the cafés are still, in a sense, out of character. In spite of it all, Cognac, as I was told by a pretty Cognaçaise, hungry for the gaieties of Angoulême, is '*très fermée*'. One can see what she means if one strolls only a stone's throw from the congested, television-loud Place François-Premier, as far as the older part of the town, where the cobbled alleys, gutters in the middle, and without pavements, sloping down to the river, are lined with houses of pale stone. It is quiet now, where once the casks rumbled down to the barges in the Charente, waiting to take the cognac to the ships at Tonnay-Charente, and the houses are *fermées* indeed, though many a Cognac family lives cosily behind the shutters.

As long ago as 1924, Curnonsky wrote that since the First World War the people of the region generally—it is even truer now, and even truer of Cognac itself—were 'going less and less to restaurants, which is why good places have become rare. They entertain you at home magnificently. . .'

And indeed they do—*en prince* at the great châteaux in which firms such as Martell and Hennessy, Rémy-Martin, Bisquit and Courvoisier dispense hospitality to friends and to customers who are treated as friends; and with similarly fine food, noble wines (claret is the wine of the region) and ancient brandies, if in more modest settings, by smaller but no less hospitable houses.

This, of course, is a reason why there is not a hotel or a restaurant in Cognac worth mentioning: one eats better, however simply, in the modest villages around. Or in Jarnac or Barbezieux, ten and twenty miles away respectively, each about a quarter the size of Cognac, but each with more style, more local pride (perhaps because they feel that Cognac is too well-known, themselves too little), so that at one good little restaurant in Jarnac they serve only the cognacs of Jarnac (Delamain, Hine, Courvoisier, Bisquit-Dubouché—they do not really deprive themselves), none of the cognacs of Cognac, and so that Barbezieux, famous for its *poulardes* and its *chapons*, its game and its fruits in brandy, and with its Michelin-starred Boule d'Or, can proclaim proudly at the entrance to the town that it is an '*Etape de Gourmandise*'.

Cognac is undoubtedly the capital of the cognac trade, but it is in Jarnac and in Barbezieux that one captures the spirit—the spirit, I mean, in its other sense: the *genius loci*—of the Charentes. Barbezieux still evokes *la douceur de vivre*, says the latest Michelin Green Guide to the region, just as it did on the very eve of the last war, when Jacques Chardonne wrote his *Le Bonheur de Barbezieux*, and as it had done thirty years before when, as Chardonne recalled, 'in a little town in the Charente, everyone was as happy as anyone can be on earth'. The Barbeziliens, now as then, still 'live in their quiet houses, looking out on to secret gardens, filled with birdsong, counting their days of peace'.

Jarnac is more of a centre for the cognac trade than Barbezieux—headquarters, indeed, of some of the greatest houses, although it is so much smaller than Cognac, and spared the racket of a main road: it is the quietly flowing Charente that bisects the little town, and that seems to impose its own pace upon its people. When Charles Morgan, writing *The Voyage* in Jarnac in the late nineteen-thirties, set his novel in the eighteen-seventies, between the Prussians' invasion of France and the phylloxera's, he knew that the streets, the houses, the trees and the river-banks looked the same to him as they had done to the characters in his book, two generations earlier. They look the same now, a generation later, as does most of the countryside.

One old regional custom, it is true, survives only in the mind's eyes of the more imaginative travel-writers, among whom for once I must include the editor of the Michelin Green Guide to the Côte de l'Atlantique. I have seen more than one vintage in the Charentes, and in 1971 I ranged the whole region, east to west and north to south, over a period of some months, including the vintage. Nowhere did I see even the oldest women wearing the *quichenotte*, the old-fashioned linen or cotton summer poke-bonnet, shading the face, the name of which is held to derive from 'kiss-not', and which is said to date from the days of English rule in Guienne.

I saw the *quichenotte* very occasionally indeed in the Médoc during the vintage of 1967, but it seems to have disappeared from the Charentes, whatever the guide-books may say.

That apart, it seems in most ways that the people of Jarnac, the people of the Charentes generally, are as slow to change as they are slow in their manner of speaking and in their habits. This may be, as we have seen, part of the Languedoc and, to that extent, of the south of France rather than the north, but there is nothing here of Provence, of the Mediterranean, no Gascon ebullience of speech or gesture. If they call themselves Gallo-Romans they are more Gaulish than Roman, or more ancient Roman than modern.

They used to be called—perhaps they still are called—'*cagouil-lards*', after the *cagouille*, the fat snail of their vineyards, and they have indeed been so slow in taking up new things that they were the last wine-growers in France to take to distilling their wines into brandy.

Slow but sure: when at last they did take to a process that had longed ceased elsewhere to be new-fangled the brandy they produced was cognac.

3. The Spirit of the Place

For centuries, the slow-moving people of this benign and smiling countryside grew wine not only for themselves and for their near neighbours, but also for the wineless and less sunny countries of the north.

And it was good wine—good enough, certainly, for Balts and Flemings, Dutchmen and Englishmen, to give shipping space to, and good money for, or the mercantile equivalent of good money. There was—and there is—no reason why a temperate and well-husbanded region lying between the Loire and the Bordelais should not produce wines at any rate comparable with those produced just to the north and just to the south.

As in other parts of western Europe, it was the Romans who brought the vine, the cultivation of which in these parts had been forbidden by the Celtic priests. The Romans also brought to the coasts of the region their Mediterranean methods of salt extraction: by the end of the tenth century, if not earlier, the production and sale of salt, corn and wine had brought prosperity to the Angoumois, Saintonge and Aunis.

By the twelfth century, these basic commodities of civilized living were being regularly exchanged, in impressive amounts, for the salt cod and salt herring, the furs and the timber, of the north, the trade being carried on largely in Flemish and Hanseatic bottoms, which called in at English ports, coming and going.

This trade with England increased when Henry II succeeded to the English throne in 1154, already the husband of Eleanor of Aquitaine, who had brought to the marriage the whole of Aquitaine, the greatest wine-growing region of France, of which the part we deal with was the northern half, and La Rochelle its port, as Bordeaux was of the southern part.

Robert Delamain has explained in his *Histoire du Cognac* (Paris, 1938) why trade to the north was brisker from these ports—but from La Rochelle particularly—than from those, more geographically convenient, of Brittany and the French channel coast. For the seafaring men of the north, landfall was more attractive, the products of the hinterland more interesting. It was not until they had rounded Ushant and turned east again, as well as south, to reach the mouth of the Loire and then the Saintonge coast—its ports of Rochefort and La Rochelle sheltered from the north by the great westward-jutting bulge of Brittany and from the wilder Atlantic storms by the islands of Ré and of Oléron—that they felt they had come at last to the south, land of fruit and wine, calmer seas than their own, and sunnier skies. And by the time of which we now speak—the mid-twelfth century and onwards—this had obtained for so long that the people of Aunis, Saintonge and the Angoumois (which for the sake of convenience I shall refer to by the present-day name of the Charentes, its people as the Charentais) were far more experienced in conducting a seaborne import–export trade than those of most other parts of France, save the Mediterranean coast.

It is from this period that not only does La Rochelle date its importance, but also Tonnay-Charente, now a ghost-port, but in those days the highest point upstream for sizeable ships, and Saintes and Cognac, which smaller ships could reach, to meet the barges coming downstream from Angoulême to collect the salt of the littoral.

Thus a pattern had been created, of trade routes along which, and of ports to which, the wines of this area were, and had long been, despatched.

And of markets, too, in which they were enjoyed, for while André Simon stated firmly[1] that throughout the Middle Ages 'we shall find the Bordeaux vintners to be by far the most numerous, the most powerful, and the wealthiest men engaged in the wine trade in England', Edmund Penning-Rowsell, able to work, nearly seventy years later, in more carefully-tilled fields of research, has shown that this was true only of the later Middle Ages—from the thirteenth century onwards. The Bordeaux area, Mr Penning-Rowsell points out, was not even mentioned among the regions exporting wine to England in King John's edict of 1199, regulating foreign trade: 'the leading suppliers came from further north, in the Poitou'.[2]

It is true that after about this time the wines shipped from Bordeaux—not yet those of the Médoc, but of St-Emilion, Blaye, the Graves, and other areas nearer to or more accessible from the city—began to acquire an increasingly dominant part of the English market, but the wines of Poitou continued to be sold in England, Ireland, Scandinavia and the Low Countries until the seventeenth century and, for the earlier part of this period at any rate, to be held in high esteem.

The so-called 'wines of St John', once thought to be the German Johannisberger, but identified by André Simon as those of St-Jean-d'Angély, south-east of La Rochelle—wines that were full and strong in those days—were supplied to Henry III and to Edward I. There are numerous mentions throughout the fifteenth century of Rochelle wines being taken from French merchantmen, bound for the Low Countries, the Baltic and Scandinavian ports, seized by the English as prizes during the Hundred Years' War; and once the wars were over, and for a century later, English wine-merchants flocked to La Rochelle, St-Jean-d'Angély and Saintes, licences being granted by Henry VIII to those who wished to import Poitevin wine. As late as

[1] Simon, *The History of the Wine Trade in England*, London, 1905-6.
[2] Penning-Rowsell, *The Wines of Bordeaux*, London, 1969, and New York, 1970.

Elizabeth's reign, an average of 6,000 tuns of wine were shipped every year from the Charente ports to England, and this was only a part of the total export.

For most of this period, until the last few decades, they were still good wines. Dutch ships were sailing as far upstream as Cognac in the 1550s, loading for Irish, Baltic and Scandinavian ports the sweet, fragrant and *pétillant* (lightly sparkling) wines of the region already called the Borderies,[3] made from the Colombard grape (still grown in the region, though to a diminishing extent, and in California, for Californian brandy).

In 1603 Etienne Thevet, surgeon to the then Prince of Conti, wrote of the medicinal virtues of the wines of Aunis:[4] the prince's contemporary, and fellow-nobleman, the great Duke of Buckingham, with the wines of the known wine-growing world to choose from, also commended the wines from La Rochelle—not, presumably, because they did him good, but because he liked the taste.

*   *   *

No other wine-growing area of similar size, commercial importance and long tradition has so completely given up the growing and the export of table wines: when and—more interesting—why did the Charentais turn instead to producing and selling brandy?

Some authors have written as though the change took place almost overnight, and some have each produced only one reason for it.

One that has been put forward, for instance, is that it occurred to the Dutch, apparently all of a sudden, that it would be cheaper to carry a spirit than the much greater bulk of the wine that it could be distilled from, and that if water were added to the spirit at the end of its journey it would thus be turned back into wine—as though adding water to whisky would make beer of it, and as though the Dutch, who had known all about schnapps and other ardent spirits for centuries, would think

[3] See chapter 5.
[4] Etienne Thevet was a native of Angoulême and nephew of the André Thevet who introduced tobacco into France, calling it *'herbe angoumoisine'*.

any such foolish thing. Or, for that matter, even if they did, would not disprove it once and for all, with a glass of brandy and a jug of water at a table, rather than send ships to sea and wait for their return to witness the failure of a miracle.

Other writers have explained the change from wine-production to brandy-production by quoting the complaints made in the middle of the seventeenth century by peasant wine-growers of the Angoumois—the deputies of Cognac and Jarnac among them—that taxes levied on wine conveyed by boat down the Charente put them at a disadvantage compared with the wine-growers of the coast: they began, it is argued, to distil their wines in desperation.

But these complaints seem to have been made when the practice of distillation was already well under way, and the evidence, in any case, is ambiguous: the complainants seem to have been those who did not want to distil, and who resented the fact that those of their neighbours who were already doing so were cutting down the trees of the region to provide firewood for their stills.

This seems to have been more of a reaction by the more conservative wine-growers against successful rivals who were moving with the times.

Then again, it is suggested—indeed, it is positively stated— that the English and the Dutch asked the people of the Charentes to distil their wines because they were too thin and sharp to travel well. But the wines of the region always *had* travelled well—for hundreds of years, indeed. What is to the point is to enquire whether the wines of the early sixteenth century differed from those of the middle ages; if so, in what way, and why. . .

It may well be that there was a decline in quality during the seventeenth century—due largely, at any rate, to the devastation caused by the religious wars of the mid-sixteenth century. The ruined vineyards had to be replanted, and the poverty-stricken vine-growers, anxious for quick returns, turned to strains more prolific than they had grown before, but that proved unsuitable for the production of decent table wine, and useful only for distillation; or that produced wines too light and thin to travel so well as those that purchasers had been used to, with the result that the purchasers themselves took to distilling them rather than suffer loss.

This part of France, particularly, was grimly fought over. Protestantism was strong in the south-west. Relatively, it still is: Jarnac is largely Protestant, as are many of its brandy families. The Cognac families are now Catholic, but in those days Cognac was a Huguenot town, held by a Huguenot garrison, and La Rochelle was the very citadel of the reformed faith. Pierre Loti, whose family name was Viaud, came from Rochefort and was of Huguenot descent.

It was at Jarnac, in 1569, that Condé 'the Huguenot Prince Rupert',[5] wounded and a prisoner, was butchered, for his corpse to be mounted on a donkey and paraded through the Catholic camp. The *croquants*, peasants made desperate by the ravishing of their fields and their females, laid waste what the Catholic and the Protestant armies had spared, and were still pillaging a generation after the Wars of Religion had broken out—pretty well to the end of the century.

So there must certainly have been a vast amount of replanting of vines in the region throughout the latter part of the sixteenth century and the first decades of the seventeenth. But it is important to remember that this was precisely the period during which the infant Dutch Republic became the chief trading country of the world—all in a mere generation from the granting of letters of marque by the Prince of Orange in 1569 to eighteen privateers—the 'sea-beggars'—to harass Spanish ships and Spanish-held ports. In spite of challenges from Cromwell's and Charles II's navies, this domination by the Dutch lasted for a century, during which 'they were the carriers whose ships brought the corn and timber from the Baltic, the wines from Spain and France, the salt from the Cape Verde Islands, to the wharves and warehouses of the Zuiderzee and the Meuse, and again distributed them to foreign markets . . . their trade with each succeeding year grew and prospered. . . . Commerce became a passion with the Hollanders and Zeelanders; and eagerness after gain by the expansion of trade possessed itself of all classes'

[5] The phrase is Desmond Seward's (*The First Bourbon*, London and Boston, 1971).

(*Cambridge Modern History* [Cambridge, 1905], volume 3, chapter XIX).

In particular, as Roger Dion has shown,[6] they dominated the wine trade from the French Atlantic coast, and Professor Dion goes on to explain in detail how skilfully they managed it. None of their ships left a Dutch port save with goods easily saleable in the country of destination. 'During the period of Dutch trade domination, there was no more to be seen the piles of ballast-stones at the moorings of ships from the north that had come to load wine and salt.' (It is significant that whereas in the Bordelais today there are churches built of Bath stone brought as ballast from Bristol in the middle ages and later, there is also a traditional local liking for Dutch cheese. The stone came from England as ballast, the cheese from more commercially-minded Holland as a trading commodity.)

The Huguenots of La Rochelle were their natural allies against Spain, and so it was all the easier for the Dutch in this part of France to employ local agents to further commercial intelligence. Many Dutch sailors married French Protestant girls.

The Dutch sought far more skilfully and, therefore, far more successfully than any traders had done before, how best to adapt their own merchandise to local requirements, and how best to increase, by appropriate treatment and refashioning in Holland, or by instruction and advice to the people from whom they bought, the value of the foreign merchandise that passed through their hands.

Thus, they taught Frenchmen improved methods of drawing and racking wine; how to fortify it for sea-voyages; and how to sweeten it with syrup to meet the tastes of the north. (As a very general rule, the inhabitants of cold countries like their wines sweeter than those of warmer climes. Look at the 'rich' champagnes that the Russian grand dukes used to drink.) Colbert wrote in 1669 that 'the Dutch come every year down [*sic*] the Garonne and the Charente with three or four thousand vessels to load wines during the months of October, November and December. They carry these wines off to their own country

[6] Roger Dion, *Histoire de la Vigne et du Vin en France des Origines au XIXe Siècle* (Paris, 1959).

. . . drink a third of them, or thereabouts; the other two-thirds are kept, improved and adulterated and then, in March or April, reloaded upon the same ships and taken to Germany, the Baltic and other northern countries where French wines are drunk.'

It seems foolish to suppose that traders as shrewd, experienced and ambitious as this discovered brandy by accident, or turned to it because for centuries they had been shipping wines that did not travel. Surely it must have been as the result of deliberate trading policy that the Dutch got the people of the lands between the Loire and the Gironde not merely to turn their wines into brandy, but to grow the right sort of grapes to do so.

One cannot but suppose that the Dutch had seen that there were great areas of western France where the wines were quite good, but not so good as those of the regions around Bordeaux; that these areas could grow more wine still, of inferior quality as table wine, but highly suitable for distillation. First, though, it was necessary to make brandy—known at the time as a medicinal cordial—into an everyday drink, in general demand.

The peoples of the foggy north are spirit-drinkers: the very climate that makes viticulture impossible calls for drinks that are cold in the mouth but warming in the veins and belly, and to the cockles of the heart. The Scotsman with his whisky bears witness, the Muscovite with his vodka, and so, too, the Dutch, who converted their own sailors, used to all sorts of north-European schnapps made from grain, into brandy-drinkers, and they in their turn made it popular in the countries to which they voyaged.

'Under Dutch influence', writes Professor Dion, 'the distillation of wine in a pot-still which, in the middle ages, was the work of the apothecary and took up only a minute part of the wine-harvest, became the peasants' task and took its place among the normal jobs relating to the harvest.'

Thus, the Dutch shipped fine wine through Bordeaux from the regions immediately adjacent, notably from what we now call the Sauternais, but from further afield they shipped brandy. Hence, indeed, the origins of Armagnac, another brandy-producing region that once exported table wine.

In the Charentes, brandy was already being made as early as the middle of the sixteenth century, especially around La Rochelle itself and to the north, in the Aunis region. Poorer wines were being grown, on a larger scale, deliberately to this end.

This form of cultivation—of prolific vines producing thin wine meant for distilling—was particularly suitable for small-holders of modest means. The Dutch paid well for a commodity cheap to produce, because it came from cheap, common vine-stocks. Moreover, the Dutch not only paid promptly, but often advanced money for the purchase of more land and of more vines to plant in it. It was especially in the regions trading with the Dutch that peasant proprietors became rich and got on in the world. It is from this period that many of the vast walled farm buildings of the region date—they must have been expensive to build, and yet they have patently never been the châteaux of even the most minor nobility: they were built by rich wine-growers.

Virtually every writer on cognac quotes Claude Masse, the engineer and cartographer, who wrote of the Charentes in 1712 that according to the oldest inhabitants of the region it was no more than ninety years since they first began to turn their wine into brandy, and that the first to set up a still to do so was a local surgeon. This puts the date at 1622 or thereabouts.

But there is a record of four casks of brandy having been shipped from La Rochelle almost a century before that, in 1529, and Professor Dion has justly observed of Masse's account that it is a typical example of oral tradition turning fact into legend—the surgeon-initiator personifies folk-memories of the time when distillation was the business of apothecaries, and popular memory reduces to the span of one long lifetime a period that was much longer: brandy production was certainly no longer in its earliest stages in 1622.

Indeed, it was beginning to succeed wine and salt as a main source of Huguenot wealth and influence in these parts before the Edict of Nantes in 1598 gave the Protestants freedom for a time to exercise their talents and energies elsewhere than in commerce.

We have seen that the establishment of the cognac trade and the pattern that it took owed much to the wars of religion—to the struggle of the Protestants of the Netherlands against Catholic Spain, and to the Protestant sympathies of the French provinces that became the Charentes.

For a long time the cognac trade was in the hands of Protestants to a degree quite out of proportion to Protestant influence elsewhere in France or in the French economy, or to percentage of population.

It was in the hands, indeed, of Protestants of the sterner sort, for the Huguenots of history and the French Protestants of today were and are Calvinist rather than evangelical in inspiration and outlook.

The Protestant *temple* in Jarnac is austerely devoid of decoration, remindful of nothing so much as of a Quaker meeting-house. Indeed, the partly Protestant origins of the cognac trade, the continuing Protestant element in its tradition, and the influence it has sometimes had on the courses that the trade has taken, are reminiscent of the connexion in Britain between cocoa and Quakerism.

It must be remembered, too, that by the time, in 1598, that the Edict of Nantes gave them, along with liberty of conscience and the right to practise their religion, a place in public life, Huguenots were used to exclusion from public affairs, and to concentration, in consequence, on commerce, as was the case, at various times, with dissenters in Britain and with Jews in various parts of Europe.

*   *   *

Jarnac, so much smaller than Cognac, and therefore so much less open to outside influences, has remained Protestant, and they will tell you in those parts that until well within living memory—up to the Second World War, perhaps—whereas the 'good' families of Jarnac and those of Cognac were certainly on friendly terms, they did not entertain each other in their houses, much less intermarry, because the Jarnac families were Protestant, the Cognac families Catholic.

Théophile Hazard—'Barbet'—*bouilleur de cru* in Jarnac in the eighteen-eighties, the central figure of Charles Morgan's novel *The Voyage*, was typical of his place, period and profession in being a Protestant, a good deal less so in having a mother who had been bred a Catholic.

The Delamains, a Jarnac firm and family, are Protestants. Originally from Saintonge, one member of the family travelled to London in 1625 as chef-de-suite to Henrietta-Maria, bride of Charles I. Deciding to stay in a country more hospitable than his own to his religion, Nicholas Delamain was knighted in 1639, and settled in Ireland as a Protestant landowner, and one of the Farmers-General of Ireland. One descendant was the Dublin potter, Henry Delamain, who was granted £100 by the Irish Parliament in 1753 for having been the first to fire delft-ware with coals, 'as well as was ever done with turf and wood'. (The Irish Georgian Group put on a splendid exhibition of his work at Castletown House, near Dublin, in 1971.) Nicholas's nephew, son of the constable of Dublin Castle, went to France in 1760, and entered the cognac trade, by marrying the only daughter of a Protestant *négociant* of Jarnac.

The Hines descend from a Dorset manufacturer of broadcloth who married the daughter of a supporter of the Duke of Monmouth who survived both Sedgmoor and Judge Jeffreys. Their son went to France, married a Delamain daughter, and set up on his own, also in Jarnac: the family has become French, but remains Protestant. (The first Catholic to set up in Jarnac in the cognac trade was the Bisquit of what is now Bisquit-Dubouché, and that was not until 1819.)

Not only were the Delamains and the Hines thus related— they were related too, by marriage, with the Protestant families of Augier and Gautier, both established very early in the trade, both now taken over, the one by Martell, the other by the liqueur firm of Bénédictine.

All these firms are old, and Augier, founded in 1643, the oldest of all still in existence (though now largely owned by the house of Seagram) was also Protestant in origin, and a Cognac, not a Jarnac house, at that.

(The first important Catholics in the cognac trade in Cognac were the Hennessys, who set up their business in 1765—and they were not French but Irish Catholics.)

The present head of the firm of Augier, Comte Burignot de

Varenne, is grandson to the daughter and only child of the last Augier to bear the name—Etienne, who died in 1874. She took her mother's religion, and so was brought up a Catholic, and married Catholic. By long family tradition, an Augier son would have been Protestant, whatever the Church might have said. Count Burignot is thus himself a Catholic, but he has told me how, through his Protestant forbears, he is connected with such families as the Robins and the Martells—for the Martells, too, were Protestant when they came to Cognac from Jersey in 1715, and became Catholic only about a century later, when a Martell married into the family of Firino, a general of the First Empire.

Before that, at the Revocation of the Edict of Nantes in 1685, some of the well-to-do Protestant merchants of La Rochelle, Cognac and Jarnac seem to have been interfered with remarkably little (Louis XIV and his advisers were sometimes perhaps as lenient with Protestants who traded prosperously abroad as, until the later years of the Nazi régime, Hitler was with some of his more usefully prosperous Jewish business houses).

All the same, one-third of the population of Jarnac left France, and although many of those who remained behind recanted in public, some continued to practise the rites of their faith in private, as old Catholic families did in England, and Jews in Spain, publicly resuming the religion of their fathers in more tolerant times, under the milder rule of Louis XV.

Thus, while Augier descendants may now sincerely believe that the family was unwaveringly Protestant until only a couple of generations ago, there is a record of an Augier family recantation at Cognac in 1685, the year of the Revocation of the Edict of Nantes. At about the same time, one Cognac Augier settled in Rotterdam, either defying the new law that forbade Protestants to leave the kingdom, or briefly becoming Catholic to do so. In either case, he was no doubt a Protestant in Rotterdam, and he certainly developed the trade that his newly Catholic brothers and cousins, still in Cognac, were already conducting in that city.

The differences between Catholic and Protestant no longer matter very much anywhere in the world, save in Northern

Ireland (if the real differences there are, indeed, religious) and we may be glad of it. But once they did in these parts, and in the Netherlands, and they had their share in the shaping of the cognac trade.

*   *   *

It seems odd to us now that the districts immediately adjacent to Cognac, already known as the Grande and the Petite Champagne, were about the last in the Charentes, much later than the La Rochelle district, to turn from the production of wine to that of brandy. But it was already well under way in the first half of the seventeenth century, and by the end of the century the vineyards of the Charentes contained virtually no vines other than those that were most suitable for producing wine for distillation.

And when the change did take place this was the district that produced the finest brandy of the region. In Aunis and on the islands, the growers went in solely for producing their brandy in the cheapest possible way. There was always ready cash waiting for their product at La Rochelle—only next door. The Cognaçais, knowing that their brandies would in any case have to be more expensive by the cost of transport to the coast, went in from the first for quality, enabled to do so by being better off for supplies of wood for heating the stills and for casks, and of water for cooling the *serpentins* (*see* page 69). And as different parts of the Cognac area were already described as 'grande', 'petite' and 'borderies', it must be assumed that the different qualities of soil were already well understood. Professor Dion quotes writers of the time to show that by the beginning of the eighteenth century the market created for brandy by the Dutch had already produced in its turn an élite of connoisseurs, educated to appreciate the finesse of different qualities of brandy. It is from this period that we date the fame of cognac.

4. 'Observingly Distil It Out'

THE brandy that the Charentais of the seventeenth century distilled for their Dutch customers was very different from the cognac of today: it was aged very little, and blended not at all. But it was distilled in precisely the same way. For the law now insists that cognac must be distilled in one way—the traditional way—and no other, and the gleaming gas-fired apparatus in the great modern distilleries of Martell or of Hennessy does not differ at all in principle from the ramshackle-looking single coal-fired still in the cobwebbed out-house of a peasant *bouilleur de cru*, which differs in its turn in no significant way from that used by his ancestor of two or three centuries ago. One wonders sometimes, visiting a peasant grower-distiller of the most modest sort, whether he is not in fact using the very same one.

To understand the method of distilling is cardinal to the

47

understanding of cognac. True, there are other factors that help to make cognac unique—grape, soil, climate, blending, ageing, and the oak from which its casks are made all contribute to its character and style. But it is also distilled differently from all other spirits—from grain whisky, from gin and vodka, from California brandy (which is distilled like grain whisky), and even from French 'grape brandies' and from armagnac, its only, and not very similar, rival in finesse and style.

The law jealously preserves the tradition and the difference, and the men of Cognac 'observingly distil it out', as Henry V before Agincourt bade his soldiers extract the soul of goodness from things evil. And it is noteworthy that Shakespeare too, like so many others, uses the word 'soul' for the product of distillation: brandy is the 'soul' of wine.

Cognac is the product of pot stills, not of the patent stills (or Coffey stills, so named because one particular and now widely-used type was invented—in 1830—by Aeneas Coffey, Inspector-General of Excise in Ireland) in which gin, grain whisky and vodka are produced.

Basically, the principle of distillation is simple, as I hope to have made clear in my first chapter. The difference between distillation by pot still and distillation by patent still, put very briefly, is this:

By a *continuous* distillation process, the patent still rectifies the alcohol as it is being separated from the water in whatever the fermented liquid may be, thus producing a strong, comparatively pure, or neutral (or what the whisky-distillers call a 'silent') spirit.

Such a spirit retains very little of those secondary characteristics of the original liquid that give flavour, and this is why the patent still, or continuous, method is used to produce gin, which requires to have its flavours added *after* distillation, and vodka, the virtue of which is precisely its tastelessness and lack of aroma. ('It leaves you breathless', was the Smirnoff vodka slogan in American advertisements, which was as much as to say that you could get stinking and not stink.)

This, too, is the reason why the Scotch of commerce is a blend of grain whisky, produced by the patent-still process, to

1. The Charentes countryside: river, watermeadow, woods and vines

2. a and b. A typical house of a well-to-do grower of the Charentes: 'vast but secretive, the great, heavy double gates . . . set into high blank walls behind which the farm and domestic buildings stand about a partly-grassed, partly-cobbled courtyard'. (*See* Chapter 2.)

give 'lightness' and 'dryness', but not much flavour or fragrance, and the flavoury, fragrant, 'heavier' malt, produced by pot still. And why a smallish, but growing body of connoisseurs prefers single malt or malts blended with each other but not with grain, as many of us used to enjoy Irish whiskeys before they, too, became blends.

The pot still, on the other hand, with its separate, non-continuous distillations (obligatory in the production of cognac), is slow in use and thus can easily be controlled, so that unwanted elements can be rejected, others put back for further distillation, but much of the character of the original liquid retained.

(The difference between cognac and armagnac, the other French brandy of distinction, is that whereas armagnac is also produced in old-fashioned pot stills, it is distilled only once, to cognac's twice, but at a lower temperature. Cognac leaves the still with an average strength of seventy degrees of alcohol, leaving thirty per cent for the congenerics, or flavoury characteristics; armagnac at fifty, leaving even more room than cognac for congenerics. Cognac is thus more delicate; armagnac retains even more of the character of the earth in which the grapes grew, of the grapes themselves and thus of the wine from which the brandy was distilled: it is racier of the soil.)

*   *   *

The *alambic charentais*—the pot-still distilling apparatus of the Charentes—consists of the furnace and the boiler itself, the *chaudière*, made of pure copper, as are all the metal parts into which the wine or the spirit comes into contact. Wine in process of distillation produces acids that attack metals, but pure copper least of all.

The legal limit to the size of a *chaudière*, laid down in 1967, is 25 hectolitres.[1] Its interior is polished to as smooth a finish as possible, for the sake of cleanliness; it is fitted inside brick walls and stands upon its brick-enclosed *fourneau*, furnace, which may be fired by coal or gas.

[1] The newest distilleries use a big pot still of some 50–100 hectolitres for the *brouillis*, or first distillation, but are obliged by the 1967 decree to use the smaller still for the *bonne chauffe*, or second distillation.

Wood was, of course, the original fuel for the furnaces of Cognac, but even the stills of the very smallest *bouilleurs de cru* are now fired by coal, as are some of the bigger but older distilleries, but there is not the degree of control that can be obtained by gas, and so coal-firing, too, is wasteful of man-power.

Oil has been tried, but its smell can be dangerous; electricity is forbidden, for the law, based on time-honoured tradition, states unequivocally that '*L'appareil de distillation dit "alambic charentais" est composé essentiellement d'une chaudière chauffée à feu nu . . .,*'[2] and electricity does not give a naked flame.

Virtually all modern distilleries are fired by gas—clean and easily controllable. They tell me at Martell that using gas instead of coal reduces man-power in the distillery itself by a half. This firm has always been a leader in technical development: its experts decided, after experiment, that they get better control as well, of course, as more economical production by using bigger *chaudières*, and now go in for capacities of 50 to 100 hectolitres (1,100 to 2,200 gallons) for the first distillation, which is four or five times as big as those they once used.

But this is only for the first boiling: as will be seen, there is a second distillation, and for this even Martell continue to use older, smaller *chaudières*, of twenty to twenty-five hectolitre capacity. Traditionalists had long argued that distillation in boilers of much more than about 400-gallon capacity meant a loss of quality: these smaller boilers for the second distillation are not appreciably bigger than this, and it is the second distillation that is the key to quality.

The *chaudière* is surmounted by a copper *chapiteau*, the head of the still, either the shape of a pear or of an olive, with a swan-neck pipe leading from it (this is the *col de cygne* form) or bigger and turban-shaped (*tête de Maure*) with a straighter pipe sloping down from it to the condenser, the tall metal drum, inside which the pipe from the *chapiteau* takes a serpentine form (the *serpentin*) and is immersed in cold running water.

In some stills a *chauffe-vin*, or *réchauffe-vin*—wine-warmer—is placed between boiler and condenser. In such stills, the hot

[2] Landrau, *Le Cognac Devant la Loi*, Montpellier, n.d.

vapour from the boiler passes through this on its way to the condenser, thus beginning its own cooling process but, more important, at the same time warming the cold new wine (up to about 45 degrees Centigrade or 113 degrees Fahrenheit) on its way from vat to boiler, thus saving time and heat.

The law, which has much to say on equipment and process, does not make the *chauffe-vin* an obligatory part of the still, and opinions differ as to its value. Most, though not all, of the old stills included one, and those firms, or individual *bouilleurs de cru*, that have inherited serviceable old stills go on making use of it. Some swear by it.

But a *chauffe-vin*, with all its brass and copper appurtenances and brick foundations, is an expensive piece of equipment—I have been told that it could account for up to thirty per cent of the total cost of a still. In any case, even in the old days, there were experts who, if they did not doubt its efficacy, nevertheless pointed out that it had to be cleaned with great care, used with great skill, and its temperature very carefully controlled, or the incoming wine could be tainted or overheated, or both, and communicate to the final distillation an oily, cooked, or scorched smell and taste.

So, one way and another, it looks as though present-day feeling in the Charentes is that when new stills are being installed the eventual savings to be made by including a *chauffe-vin* are outweighed by the initial cost, the interest on it, and the extra attention it demands. On the other hand, those that are already installed are good things to have, for those who know how to use them.

Martell got rid of their last *chauffe-vin* more than half a century ago: now, none of their stills has one. Hennessy and the big Unicoop co-operative that produces Prince Hubert de Polignac cognac have them in existing stills but are not including any in their gleaming new installations. At the other extreme, the two elderly coal-fired stills that Monsieur Marcel Ragnaud inherited along with his hundred acres of vines, and the family business, have no *chauffe-vins*, either, so it is clearly not a new-fangled notion to do without. At the same time there are many distinguished distillers, Salignac, particularly, and Camus among them, who still swear by the method—clearly, because they know well how to use it. It is not the only instance, as we shall see, where distillers (and blenders, for that matter) differ, yet where the consumer finds no difference in the final product— precisely because the producers know their jobs, whichever way they choose to go about them.

*   *   *

It is laid down by law, and by tradition that is even stronger than the law, that there are two separate distillations in the production of cognac. (So it is naughtily misleading for a cognac house to advertise that it is 'distilled twice over to be extra smooth': it is distilled twice over, like all other cognacs, because the law requires it.)

The first distillation is the *première chauffe*, or the *chauffe de vin*.

The new wine, usually still with its lees, but not with too much, is pumped from its fermentation vat into the boiler, and brought slowly, over a period of some couple of hours, to 76 degrees Centigrade (169 degrees Fahrenheit), this being the temperature at which alcohol vaporizes (water vaporizes at 100 degrees). The vaporized alcohol travels through the tube to the *serpentin* in the condenser—by way, if there is one, of the *chauffe-vin*, warming the incoming wine as it does so and thus also losing some of its own heat, and beginning the work of the condenser.

Condensed by cooling, the alcoholic vapours become liquid alcohol again—the so-called *brouillis*, the cloudy first part of which, the *produit de tête*, about one to one-and-a-half per cent of the total, is set on one side: it carries disagreeable smells and flavours, and needs further rectification.

Now comes the heart of the *brouillis*, so-called, indeed, in French—*le coeur*: about sixty per cent of the total. It is colourless, and virtually without smell or taste.

The run from the condenser to the tank or reservoir is cut when the alcoholometer shows that the degree of alcohol is dropping below about five degrees: the thirty-eight or thirty-nine per cent still to come is the *produit de queue*. This 'tail' is also set aside, like the 'head'. The head goes into the next new wine and is thus distilled twice again; the tail into the next *brouillis*, and will be distilled once more. (The residual water may not nowadays be simply thrown away, lest it cause pollution to local streams and rivers. It must first be treated.)

It takes three of these first distillations to produce enough heart to make the *bonne chauffe*, or second distillation—a matter of about eight hours in all.

The *chaudiere* is cleaned, and in go the 'hearts' of the three *brouillis*. This time the period of distillation is longer—twelve hours or so—and again there are 'heads' and 'tails', though they account for a much smaller proportion of the whole than in the first distillation. Again, they are set aside and put back, to be redistilled yet again with the next *brouillis*.

There is a pleasant smell, as of jam-making, during the first distillation, as I discovered at the Salignac distillery in St-Jean-d'Angély, but the first run of spirit, the head of the *brouillis*, tastes pretty nasty, as does the long tail. The heart tastes barely at all, though it is far from being a neutral spirit.

The second run is another matter. I was at Hennessy's vast new distillery at Le Peu for the opening of the distilling season in November 1971. Distilling in a modern distillery is an un-dramatically austere, almost clinically clean, process. Waiters and waitresses were laying tables for a banquet to be given that evening to the *préfet*, while distillers watched the colourless second distillation gently trickling from the condenser through a felt filter into its cask. The fragrance was intense: a friend with me, long resident in Germany, and used to the colourless fruit *eaux-de-vie* of the Black Forest, exclaimed how much it smelled like *himbeergeist*, the wild-raspberry schnapps that the French call *eau de vie de framboise*. Hennessy's man clapped his hands delightedly: 'Of course', he cried, 'it's the smell of the vine in flower.'

But on the tongue it was liquid dynamite—seventy degrees, Gay-Lussac, which is to say nearly twenty-five 'over-proof' in British terms, or nearly twice the strength of the spirits we are used to.

It is at this point, though, that one can begin to call 'cognac' what has hitherto been at first a thin wine and then a crude spirit, and it is a dedication of distillers, if one may coin a collective noun, that has effected this minor miracle.

For in spite of the greater measure of control and reduction in man-power made possible both by gas-firing and by the installation of ever bigger *chaudières*, it is human skill and experience that counts.

It takes some eight hours, which must not be interrupted, for the first of the three stages of the first distillation to be completed. The coal fire must be tended, or the control panel of the gas-fired apparatus watched, so that the heat remains constant, and there must be expert tasting of the spirit, and watching of the alcoholmeter, so that the head of the distillate can be separated from the heart, and the heart from the tail.

So, too, after three such distillations, with the *bonne chauffe*, during which there has to be a regulated flow of spirit, and a regulated variation of heat.

However up to date the distillery and its apparatus, there is no substitute for human skill, in a vast number of instances passed on from father to son. In every distillery, there is a little bedroom where the little team of two or three *distillateurs* can doss down in turn for an hour or so while the long vigil goes on that has at last produced cognac, though it is still cognac in its crudest and most basic form.

What will transform it from this deliciously fragrant but terrifyingly potent firewater into the subtle, life-enhancing liquor that *we* think of as cognac—cognac in its finished form, so to speak—is ageing and blending, together with some other, only marginally important, processes.

Chiefly, ageing and blending.

5. Vineyard and Vine

Before, though, we see how the raw young spirit is aged and blended, we must go back to consider the wine from which it is distilled, and the limited area from which it comes.

When, on 1 May 1909, the French government formally delimited the area, the brandy from which alone was to be entitled to the *appellation controlée* 'cognac', it merely gave as it were an official seal to practices that had long been observed by producers and understood by consumers.

Long been observed and understood by them, but more recently abused by others.

As Morton Shand explained,[1] the growing shortage of finer wines that resulted from the devastation of the phylloxera, which first struck the vineyards of the Charentes in 1878, and ravaged them for four years, 'produced a flood of mendacious labels which either cloaked mixtures of cheap foreign wines or else chemically "improved" common French ones. Although an

[1] Shand, *A Book of French Wines*, revised and edited by Cyril Ray, London, 1964.

enormous acreage of former vineyards was definitely abandoned, the reconstruction of the remainder with grafted vines proved terribly costly, and the hard-hit owners clamoured for prohibition of the sale of wines having no title to their names.'

The law of 1909 provided for the territorial delimitation of appellations of origin, and that of cognac was based upon local knowledge, the custom of the trade, and various official, unofficial and semi-official classifications of the component zones of the region that had been made throughout the nineteenth century, but never given the force of law.

The *eau-de-vie* of the region was known as 'cognac' in England as early as 1687, when '76 Pieces of Conyack Brandy' were offered for sale in the *London Gazette*,[2] and throughout the eighteenth and nineteenth centuries, as we shall see. The new delimitation confirmed the connoisseur in what he already knew: the best brandy came from the area now officially entitled to give its product the name 'cognac'.

Similarly, although it was not until 1936 and 1938 that the sub-divisions of the *appellation controlée* region of 1909 were given the form in which we know them today, these various enactments merely gave official sanction, legal protection, and a precise delimitation to variations of quality according to place that had been recognized for a couple of centuries.

The fundamental division in the region between districts growing good, better and best wines for the production of cognac is between *champagne*[3] and *bois*—between meadow and woodland respectively.

[2] I take my quotation from the *Oxford English Dictionary* which, by a happy chance, also provides an illustration of the abuses that followed the phylloxera, and that led to the delimitation of 1909. It quotes from the *Pall Mall Gazette* of 21 June 1882, 'Cognac in large quantities now enters England which comes out of potatoes and not out of grapes. Pure cognac can now be secured . . . only through English holders of old stocks.'

[3] The connection between, on the one hand, what we shall see are now two Champagne sub-districts of the region and, on the other, that part of France, once the province of Champagne, whence the wine of that name comes, is precisely the same as that with the Italian word *campagna* and the English 'champaign', found in Shakespeare and Milton and Tennyson, as signifying open country, not wooded or mountainous.

Delamain points out that the 'Grande Champagne de Cognac' is referred to as early as 1713 in a protest of parish priests against what they regarded as over-heavy taxation.[4]

This is of interest as establishing a sub-regional name, and I have been told of, but not seen for myself, documents of about the same period that refer to a 'Petite Champagne'.

Nor, for that matter, can I altogether agree with Delamain in assuming as a matter of course that the 1713 mention of the Grande Champagne had no geographical or administrative connotation, but referred only to quality of the vines. It seems to me likely enough that the troublesome priests could have given their address, or been referred to, as 'of the villages in that big meadow region near Cognac'.

All the more so, as it is not until about a century later that we find any brandy of the region described as coming from the Bois.

What seems to me much more probable is that the Grande Champagne and the Bois districts were recognized as such first, just as in Kent we refer to a village as being in the Weald, or the Marsh, or on the Downs, and that as growers and distillers and shippers came increasingly to recognize differences in quality between the brandies of the region, they learned to relate these to the geographical sub-divisions already established.

However that may be, the middle nineteenth century found the growers, brokers and shippers of the region, and their customers, formulating 'classifications', based on, and in their turn therefore a basis for, price, just as had happened rather earlier in the Bordelais, so that the committee charged in 1855 with the classification of the wines of the Gironde was able to draw upon a century of recorded experience.[5]

There was already a great deal of commercial experience behind the 1861 map of the various sub-districts of the region and the 1874 *Dictionnaire des crus*,[6] and in 1875 a group of British

[4] op. cit.

[5] Cyril Ray, *Lafite: The Story of Chateau Lafite-Rothschild*, London and New York, 1968: chap. 3, 'The Classification'.

[6] A *'cru'* is a 'growth' and, by extension, a region or area in which the 'growth' of vine and wine has a discernible character of its own. The Gironde classification of 1855 is divided into five *'crus'*.

shippers further sub-divided the sub-divisions into no fewer than sixteen qualities.

In 1876, when the phylloxera had barely yet struck the cognac region, Bertall, gathering material for the book he published in 1878, and for the drawings some of which decorate this book, recorded four so-called 'categories' or 'qualities' as forming the '*géographie cognacicole*' of the Charentes: with one further sub-division, and an allowance for a furthest-flung region that in practice is of small importance, they are the same as the six *crus* we know to-day, firmly delimited by law.

As they lie in more or less concentric circles, it is proper enough to refer to them as 'zones', and it is convenient to list them here not only with their geographical positions, but each with a note on the character of its soil and of the brandy that its wine produces. In descending order of importance, and of the price commanded, they are:

GRANDE CHAMPAGNE

This is an area of some 90,000 acres, about half of it, but two-thirds of its cultivable area, under vines approved for distillation, comprising 27 communes, lying south of Cognac and Jarnac, with the river Charente as its northern boundary, its modest tributary, the Né, on the west and south and, on the east, falling just short of the road from Jarnac to Barbezieux by way of Châteauneuf-sur-Charente.

This is the zone with the chalkiest soil of a chalky region, and the mildest sub-climate in a region of mild climates. Its wines, when distilled, produce what is the most delicately subtle and fragrant of cognacs and yet the one most suitable for ageing: it takes longer in wood than the others to reach its peak, but the peak is higher and it stays there longer.

PETITE CHAMPAGNE

This zone partly embraces the Grande Champagne with a southern semi-circle: it consists of sixty communes, and is almost exactly twice the size of the Grande Champagne, but only a third of its cultivable area is under approved vines, as against two-thirds of that of the Grande Champagne. Its western

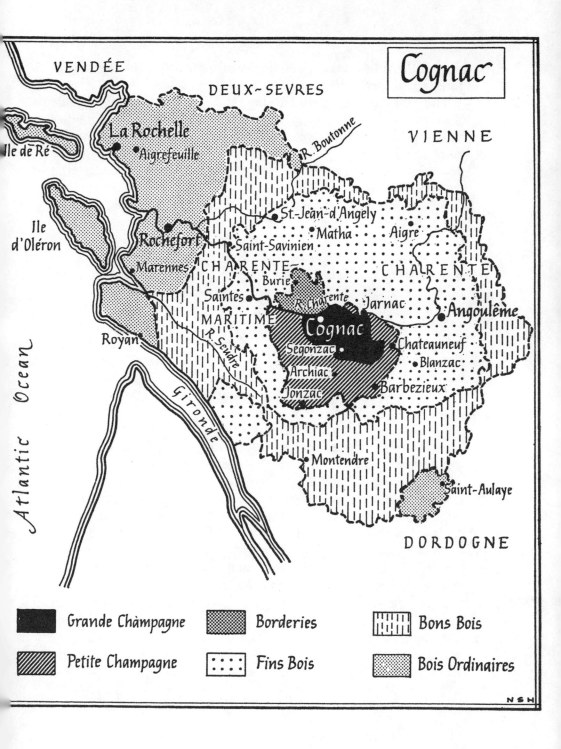

and southern boundary sweeps in a curve roughly through Pons, Jonzac and Barbezieux.

The sub-climate is much the same as that of the Grande Champagne, but the chalky soil is rather less friable. Its brandies closely resemble those of the Grande Champagne, but mature more quickly. Perhaps another way to put it would be to say that with the same length of time in cask they never reach quite the same finesse.

All the same, the difference is marginal and the Petite Champagne brandies are very highly regarded and fetch a high price, especially as only about the same amount is available. Those from around Archiac are especially renowned, and fetch pretty well Grande Champagne prices; if there were to be a reclassification, the Grande Champagne might well push out a southern salient to take in Archiac.

The two Champagnes are so close in quality that they are bracketed together in defining the *appellation* 'Fine Champagne'. For a cognac to be permitted to call itself Fine Champagne it must consist only of brandies from these two zones, and of at least fifty per cent Grande Champagne.

BORDERIES

Smallest of the zones, consisting of only ten communes—only 33,500 acres, compared with the Grande Champagne's 90,000, and the Petite Champagne's 170,000—this lies to the north of Cognac itself and the Charente, immediately contiguous to the Grande and Petite Champagnes on the south and otherwise enclosed within a semi-circle of the next zone, the Fins Bois.

Its sub-climate is more affected than that of its two superiors by sea air; it is more wooded, and its soil is less completely chalky; its brandy is both sweeter and racier of the soil than those of the Champagnes. It is full-bodied and matures quickly and, as we shall see later, is much in demand to give backbone to a delicate blend. In consequence, the Borderies has a higher proportion of its cultivable area under approved vines than any other—no less than sixty-three per cent.

FINS BOIS

This, the biggest of the zones, covers very nearly a million acres, comprises 278 communes, and completely encircles the first three, stretching from Saintes in the west to beyond Angoulême in the east, and from St-Jean-d'Angély in the north-west to Montmoreau in the south-east, with a small, cut-off enclave to the south-west between Mirambeau and the right bank of the Gironde.

We are in the area now where, although good brandy is made that fetches a good price, it has become less important than in the first three zones. So there is more mixed farming, and there are parts of the zone that find other crops more profitable than the vine. So only fourteen per cent of its cultivable area is under vines—only twelve per cent under vines qualified for distillation into cognac.

It is a zone, too, within which there are wider variations of quality than in the Champagnes and the Borderies, so that, for instance, whereas the vineyards thin out considerably as you drive from Jarnac to Angoulême and, even more, beyond, they are as concentrated around Blanzac as in the three inner zones, for this is a good small sub-zone, and its growers have made representations lately that by virtue of the quality of their wines they should be reclassified into the Petite Champagne.

Alfred de Vigny had a family property here, Maine-Giraud, near Blanzac, inherited by his mother in 1827, which made good brandy that was usually sold to Hennessy, and at a good price. De Vigny stayed there at various times from 1848 to his death in 1867.

The soil here is looser and more pebbly; the Fins Bois brandies, although, as we have seen, they vary between themselves more than the Champagnes do, or the Borderies, can be very good. They age more quickly than their betters, which means that a youngish Fins Bois can give mellowness to similarly young, but less mature, Champagnes and Borderies in a blend.

BONS BOIS

Just as the Fins Bois encircles the small inner three zones, so the Bons Bois encircles the Fins Bois. Except for the undistinguished coastal zone of Bois Ordinaires to the west, and for two tiny enclaves (one of them, the detached part of the Fins Bois that lies on the bank of the Gironde, has already been mentioned) its boundaries are those of the Cognac *appellation controlée* region itself. With the Bois Ordinaires (see below) it covers a million acres, most of them cultivable.

This is a zone of earthier, less chalky soil that produces brandies that are thinner in quality, yet coarser in flavour than those of the inner zones. Some of the big firms turn up their noses at them, making a point of buying nothing inferior to Fins Bois; others claim that a good distiller can distil the commonness out of Bons Bois brandy, and that its plebeian vigour can indeed be of benefit to a blend. The proof of the pudding, though, is that less than twelve per cent of the zone is under vines of any sort, and less than nine per cent under cognac vines.

The manufacturers of the cheapest cognacs, such as one finds in French supermarkets, probably rely entirely or almost entirely on the Bons Bois, for there is not a great deal produced in the last, least distinguished and cheapest zone, the Bois Ordinaires.

(These supermarket cognacs are unknown in Britain and, so far as I know, in the United States. The duty on them is as high as on the finest cognacs of the most famous houses, so the price differential is trifling, and they are not worth importing. The so-called 'grape brandies' from France, but not from Cognac or Armagnac, are better value.)

BOIS ORDINAIRES

Sometimes officially referred to as Bois Ordinaires et Bois Communs and including what was once, I think, a very small sub-zone, the Bois à Terroir. In effect, the maritime area of La Rochelle, Rochefort, Marennes, and Royan, along with the islands of Ré and Oléron—a region of commonplace cognac, and not much of it. It is pretty well as profitable here to make wine as to make brandy, and it is significant that of the little more than five per cent of the cultivable area under vines, only a half is under vines for cognac.

I have drunk local wine at Marennes and La Rochelle and on both the islands—a light red wine from the Ile de Ré co-oper-

ative, sold under the brand-name, Le Petit Sergent, is served as a
'*petit vin*' at Guy Epaillard's splendid Michelin-starred Au Vieux
Port restaurant in La Rochelle, and although there is no Oléron
red, Curnonsky wrote kindly of a Côtes d'Oléron white, and I
too have sipped a rather thin island white and a bland rosé at the
zinc of the pleasant Bar André in St-Pierre-d'Oléron.

All were agreeable enough, in the circumstances, but none was
anything to write home about. The local cognac even less so: I
have tasted it at the Bar André, and bought it in St-Pierre-d'Oléron at 14 francs a bottle, when the next cheapest cognac—
Chastagne three-star, a brand unknown in Britain and the United
States, produced by a co-operative—was 17.50 francs in the
Prisunic in the middle of Cognac, and Martell three-star 27 francs
there, 25.50 at the Co-op.

It was drinkable—more so than a brandy from outside
France—but thinner and with less character or fragrance than
the three-star cognacs we know. In Ile de Ré they do not produce
a cognac of their own: what wine they do not bottle as such they
send to a mainland co-operative for distillation—some may well
have found its way into that Chastagne I bought at the Prisunic.

They say that the island wines are unsuitable or, at any rate,
not highly desirable for distilling into cognac partly because the
soil is sandy, not chalky, partly because the seaweed used to
manure the vineyards imparts a taste to the spirit. I cannot say
I have ever detected the seaweed taste, but there is no question
about the inferiority of the Bois Communs brandies.

*　　*　　*

Any of these zones is entitled to the name 'cognac' for the
spirit distilled from its wine provided, as we have seen, that
the distillation is carried out according to the prescribed method,
in the prescribed still, and provided, too, that the wine is white,
pressed from the grapes of certain prescribed types of vine—the
so-called 'noble' grapes.

The law restricts the cognac *appellation* to wine distilled from
eight varieties of vine: the St-Emilion des Charentes, the Folle-
Blanche, the Colombar, the Blanc-Ramé, the Jurançon Blanc,
the Montils, the Semillon and the Sauvignon.

Not, though, to an equal extent. Only the first three—the St-Emilion, the Folle-Blanche and the Colombar—are permitted unrestricted use; the others are tolerated only up to ten per cent each in any one crop.

In practice, virtually all cognac these days—perhaps ninety-five per cent—is distilled from the wine of the so-called Saint-Emilion grape—a misleading name, for it has no connection with the claret of St-Emilion, made—not all that far away—from Merlot and Cabernet. No one seems to know how the St-Emilion of the Charentes got its name. (It is apparently the same plant as the Ugni Blanc of the Midi and the Procanico of Elba and if, as most experts hold, this is in fact the Trebbiano of Italy, then it probably came originally from Emilia-Romagna, and was named after the river Trebbia, which cuts into the hills south of Piacenza.)

As recently as 1900, Ravaz was writing that the St-Emilion would never play more than a secondary part in cognac—it produced a good brandy, it is true, but drier and less fragrant than that of the Folle-Blanche, and with a shorter 'finish' in the nose and the mouth.

There are still old hands in the Charentes who have told me what a pity it is that they had gradually to give up the Folle-Blanche (which is the same as the Piquepoule of Armagnac) and that the St-Emilion will never give quite so elegant a cognac. Before the phylloxera, the Folle-Blanche had been by far the dominant grape, having gradually replaced the Colombar, more truly native to the region, and the grape that had made its fine exportable wines, before it took to distilling.

After the phylloxera, though, the Folle-Blanche did not take kindly to being grafted on to American root-stock, as all French vines now have to be. It became more sensitive to frost and to a disease known as 'grey rot'.

Besides being resistant to these, the St-Emilion has shown itself more desirable in other ways: it gives a bigger yield and is more regular in cropping.

What is more, it flowers and fruits later, and this is an advantage in a region which gets the majority of its *vendangeurs* most easily after they have finished picking in Bordeaux, and yet

3. a. Typical cognac still with the *chauffe-vin*—the big onion-shaped vessel between the olive-shaped *chapiteau* and the cylindrical condenser

b. A still without a *chauffe-vin* with the turban-shaped *chapiteau* connected directly with the condenser

4. Oaks in the Forest of Tronçais. (*See* Chapter 6 for a discussion of the difference in growth and texture between the timber of these slender trees and that of the sturdy Limousin oak which precisely resembles that of the English woodland.)

likes to pick its grapes a little short of perfect ripeness—good cognac needs to be made from thin, sharp wine.

(The Cognac Viticultural Station has been conducting successful experiments with a Folle-Blanche–St-Emilion hybrid: it may already have been granted restricted admission to the list of 'noble' grapes.)

There is no restriction in the Cognac region, as there is in Champagne, say, or in the Bordelais, on yield per acre, or on methods of pruning. Where table wines are grown, flavour and sugar-content—which means, eventually, alcohol content— must be sought for and maintained, even at the cost of a low yield. But for cognac, much flavour in the grape is not desirable (which is why such varieties as the muscat are banned) and only a low alcohol content is needed. This, too, is why the grapes are picked a little before full maturity.

In 1972, for instance, it was a matter for congratulation that while the quantity of wine produced was up on previous years, the percentage of alcohol in the wine was only seven, as against nine in 1971.

This lower percentage of alcohol was of advantage, because although a larger amount of wine had to be distilled to produce the same amount of brandy, meaning a lower production and a higher price, it also resulted in a greater concentration of the bouquet.

It meant, too, that acidity was higher, and acidity stimulates the reaction between the wood of the cask and the spirit it contains, thus helping maturation—the cognac becomes older quicker, as it were.

Whilst it must be remembered that the *appellation* applies to cognac, not to the wine it is made from—there are no *appellation controlée* Charentais wines, as such—nevertheless there are restrictions as to the wine itself in so far as failure to observe them affects the final product.

Thus, irrigation is forbidden, save for new vine-stocks in their first year, and so too is chaptalization—sugaring of the must to increase alcohol-content.

Generally speaking, though, in spite of the fact that there is less official control here of the way the vineyards are managed (except for new planting, which is limited), the vigneron's year is pretty much the same here as everywhere else in France: he plants new vines where he may and when he must, he turns the earth so that the rain may reach the roots; he weeds and prunes and sprays; worries about frosts in May, and counts the days from the flowering in June to work out when the vintaging will begin.

Till then, if he is a small man, he and his family are on their own. If it is one of the big properties owned by a famous shipper the small team of permanently employed vignerons will cope. But with the vintage in come the itinerants, as they used to come to the Kentish hopfields—factory-hands from the towns, gypsies, undergraduates and, more and more, the gangs of Spaniards, recruited from a central agency, who stick together, working as teams that make a three-month or even four-month job of it by beginning in the vineyards of Roussillon in August, going on to the Bordelais to pick ripe red grapes for claret and the overripe white grapes for Sauternes, turning up here in the Charentes in October and November, and then moving on for the sugar-beet.

The vintage in the Charentes always runs late: the St-Emilion, as we have seen, is a slow ripener. And even though it is picked rather short of perfect ripeness, the vintage does not usually open until well after the beginning of October, and is always going on somewhere in the region into November.

In 1971 it was not only later than Bordeaux, which is, after all, farther south, but later than Burgundy and even than Champagne. It was on 9 October that I visited Gaston Raffoux's forty-acre farm in the Fins Bois to see him begin to pick his St-Emilion grapes for brandy. So far, he had already picked the black grapes for the red wine that he drinks at his own table; some of his neighbours in a smaller way of wine-growing had begun as early as 1 October; but most of the biggest vineyards would not begin for some days.

The smaller a grower you are, the earlier you begin: you can less well afford to take risks with the weather and, more important, you may want to get hold of some grape-picking labour before it goes off to Martell or Hennessy. You may want to go there yourself.

The picking team was pretty typical of this kind of farm: three Muslim Tunisians, resident in France, who picked up jobs where they could; three fairground workers who came every year after their season was over; four neighbours from the village; and the members of the family—Papa Raffoux, his two sons and their wives; his daughter with her father-in-law; Mère Raffoux; and the octogenarian grandmother. The two older women were in the kitchen, sometimes helped by the younger ones; the men at the vines.

A nearby cottage had been rented for the month to house the workers, who were also fed, except for the Muslims, who looked after themselves. I know how they fed, because that day I took my midday meal with the family and the workers, waited on by mother and grandmother—soup made from their own tomatoes, with vermicelli; a cold fish salad (*lotte*, I think) with more tomatoes; mutton-stew with potatoes and herbs; two soft local cheeses, served with cornichons and great, crusty loaves, which everyone hacked at with clasp knives, and then, as is the custom hereabouts, the same bread with Charentais butter and home-made jam as a pudding. The meal washed down with the previous year's red wine, only 8½ degrees in strength, very soft and fruity, like a young Beaujolais, and followed by coffee and a glass of the distiller-grower's own pale Fins Bois cognac.

After lunch we were back again at the vines with our secateurs, snipping the firm green bunches from the vines, five-feet high in this vineyard, which is higher than in the Médoc and Champagne, but not so high as was traditional in these parts or as is now becoming customary again. Six feet is becoming the usual height: it makes picking easier, and is a safeguard against ground frosts.

A few days later, although in the same Fins Bois region, I was at the other extreme of sophistication from this vintage *chez Raffoux,* being vouchsafed a glimpse of the future.

In one of the vineyards that surround Bisquit-Dubouché's Château de Lignères, I saw grapes being picked by machine—by the only American Chisholm and Ryder mechanical picker in the region and, at that time, one of the only five in all France. The other four were at work, also experimentally, in the south.

In a book I had written only the year before, about a champagne, I had said that 'to pick grapes the human hand is necessary; picking-machines may be all very well for hops, but even if they could be adapted to picking grapes how could they fail to damage the bloom on their skins? And the bloom is the natural yeasts that bring about fermentation.'[7]

The bloom is more important in Cognac than in Champagne, for in Cognac it is forbidden to add yeast lest its taste remain in the brandy, whereas in Champagne yeast is always added, and legitimately.

Needs must, though, when the devil drives. It is more difficult every year to find pickers. Harder for the small growers, like Gaston Raffoux, who are the backbone of the cognac business, than for the big firm that can provide dormitories and modern amenities. (Even Bisquit-Dubouché's vast vineyards provide only thirty per cent of that enterprising firm's annual requirements of wine; a hundred small peasant-growers between them provide the rest.)

The machine I saw was being tried out, simply, as such machines have been tried out in the region for the past five years or so. Everyone was agreed that it will have to be refined before it comes into general use. It does a thorough job of getting the grapes off the vine, by what seems a feverish agitation of the branches, but there is a fair amount of bruising—more, at any rate, than is generally acceptable.

Everyone, though, is equally agreed that machine-picking will become general, at any rate in most of the vineyards of the Charentes, and sooner rather than later. The small growers will probably share the rent of machines, or perhaps the big cognac houses that have vineyards will arrange to pick for their small suppliers as well as themselves, while those without vineyards may lend money for machines.

It may be that the growers of the finest clarets and champagnes will be the last to come round to mechanical picking—they are better able than most to carry the constantly increasing cost of hand-picking, and probably the most concerned about the

[7] Ray, *Bollinger, the Story of a Champagne*, London, 1971.

condition in which their grapes reach the presses. And by the time they do come round, machines may have been so modified, or newly devised, as to be gentler in their handling of the grapes, without being less effective.

That all wine-growers will have to come round to it some time, I am sure. Costs are rising every year, and a high proportion of a wine-grower's overheads are accounted for by pickers' wages, food and, often enough, rented accommodation, or more pay in lieu. In Champagne, in 1970, I found that every one of Bollinger's 300 pickers took home between £25 and £50 (between about $60 and $120), as well as having been fed for a fortnight like a fighting-cock, and given a couple of bottles of fizz as a parting present.

Small firms and less fashionable areas pay less—and find it all the harder to get pickers at all.

So mechanical picking will have to come. It may well come sooner in the Charentes than elsewhere. It is true that the St-Emilion grape is attached strongly to its vine and does not fall off so easily, as American grapes do, when disturbed by the flailing arms of the machine. Thus, it would be more likely to be bruised were it not that it is gathered rather short of full ripeness, so that it is firm, and does not bruise or break easily. In any case, this is a country of small peasant-growers, for whom labour is difficult to find and to afford; except for the yeast on the skins, the condition of the grapes on arrival at the presses is not perhaps so important as in the champagne or the claret country. And time does not merely march on, these days, any more than a modern army does: it travels by machine.

* * *

There is no such thing in the Charentes as a 'vintage' year. For the reasons given, a high yield of what would be regarded elsewhere as a thin acid wine is welcomed.

In any case, distillation makes altogether a different thing of the wine that goes into the still, and by the time that varying ages of brandy, probably from different areas, have been blended, the character of any one particular year is neither here nor there.

As in Champagne, a coarse wine from one vineyard or area can give backbone or body to one that is fine but too delicate; a poor year's wine can give finesse to one that is too full-bodied.

*   *   *

The grapes go off the presses, which the law requires to be of a particular kind—the 'Archimedes' or continuous press is forbidden, because it crushes stalks and pips, which would release oils and other substances the taste of which would remain in the spirit after distillation. The horizontal press is used for the first pressing, which produces the '*vin de goutte*'. Then skins, pips and stalks go to a hydraulic press for a very gentle pressing to extract the remaining juice without crushing pips and stalks. This second lot of must is added to the first, and all transferred to the fermenting vessels—whether the huge concrete tanks of the big firms or the wooden casks of the small farmer.

Fermentation begins in a day or two and may take anything from a week or a fortnight to complete, according to the weather. Then the young greenish-white wine, fruity, yet dry and sharply acid, very weak in alcohol, goes to the distillery as quickly as possible and still on its lees for the first stage of its transformation—to have the heart taken out of it.

6. Heart of Oak

COGNAC, then, is made from rather thin, rather sharp wine, low in alcohol, and we have seen that there are no 'vintage' years as such. But, within these limits, if the year has been good, with the right amount of sunshine to make the right amount of sugar in the grape, though not too much (which in its turn makes alcohol in the wine, though again not too much)—then, it takes about eight or nine casks of wine to make one of cognac. (A cask in Cognac holds about sixty-six gallons.) In a poor year it can take as much as ten.

Even so, this is to begin with. The contents of that one cask will dwindle as the cognac gains character in wood.

*　　*　　*

In round figures, there are 35,000 growers in the Charentes, most of whom do not distil their wine at all, but sell it to those who do—to one of the twenty-five co-operatives, or one of the 240 small distilleries, which sell the spirit they produce to one or more of the 250 *négociants* with brand or house names, and which own distilleries. (Some of the best-known names are those of shippers that do not distil at all—they buy and blend.)

For the sake of clarity, we shall refer henceforth to these *négociants* as 'shippers', although not all of them do in fact ship their brandies abroad. At the time of writing, 167 of the 250 shippers are actually exporters.

Of the 35,000 white-wine growers already mentioned, some 5,000 keep their wine to drink at home; the rest produce wine for cognac. Forty per cent of these own less than one hectare of vines apiece.

Of the 30,000 producers of wine for cognac, 2,000 are *bouilleurs de cru*, permitted to distil their own wine but not anyone else's. There are also 300 *bouilleurs de profession*, permitted to distil not only their own wine but to buy wine for distillation and also to distil for other growers who then take back their *eau-de-vie* for maturing.

Production of cognac is:
    64 per cent by *bouilleurs de profession*
      (45 per cent on their own account)
      (19 per cent for others to mature)
     9 per cent by the co-operatives
    27 per cent by the *bouilleurs de cru*
The sale of cognac to the public is:
    94 per cent by the big shippers
    5 per cent by co-operatives
    1 per cent by *bouilleurs de cru*

But the distillers—the big firms with household names, which is to say the shippers, and the smaller firms who may well sell to them—mature a much greater amount of cognac than they have themselves distilled. Ageing is an expensive process: casks are dear, money has to be tied up for a long time, and expensive brandy is lost by evaporation in the meantime.

It is too expensive a business for most grower–distillers, and for most of the smaller distillers, to go into on a big scale, though they all keep some casks against a rainy day.

There is probably no such person as a completely typical small *bouilleur de cru*, but one whom I take to be fairly so is Monsieur

Gaston Raffoux of the hamlet of Bréville, a dozen miles from Cognac, with whom I spent a day during the vintage of 1971. He grows his own grapes on a forty-acre farm (including some black ones so that he can have a glass of his own red wine at his own table); he makes his own wine; and he distils his own brandy in his one, old-fashioned still.

Incidentally—and in this, at any rate, I gather that he is typical of his kind—he never speaks of 'cognac', only of *eau-de-vie*. Until the First World War, or thereabouts, this was general throughout the region, even among the big shippers. It is natural enough, I suppose. The only brandy a Charentais knows is cognac—no need, therefore, specifically to call it cognac. Come to think of it, a Scotsman talks of whisky, not of Scotch; a Bordelais not of Bordeaux, or of claret, but of wine.[1]

Monsieur Raffoux sells virtually all the cognac he makes, after a couple of years in wood, save for a little to be drunk at home. Samples go out, and he sells where he can, but most is taken as it has been for years, by a middleman who sells to Hennessy.

Monsieur Raffoux will probably not disagree with me and certainly not be hurt if I say that he is a typical peasant—he eats in the kitchen, collarless and in his shirtsleeves (better, as I shall show later, than any stockbroking family in the Home Counties colour-supplement country), and his house has no running water or indoor sanitation.

But he buys a new Mercedes every two years, and his wife, son and daughter-in-law, all, of course, involved in running the farm, have each their own cars, too.

Another *bouilleur de cru* with whom I spent a day lives a far more sophisticated life, with family portraits on the walls and Vieux Château Certan 1964 on the dinner-table, followed by Gaffelières-Naudes 1959 (it would be a rare host in this part of the world who had burgundy at his table), before coming to his own thirty-five-year-old Grande Champagne Grande Réserve.

For Monsieur Marcel Ragnaud inherited a hundred acres at

[1] Generally speaking, the custom in the trade seems to be to refer to the full-strength, unblended spirit as either *eau-de-vie* or 'cognac', indifferently, but to the reduced and blended product only as 'cognac'.

Ambleville, in the heart of the Grande Champagne district of Cognac, along with a couple of stills, and fine stocks of old brandy. He not only sells very profitably, but has made an enviable reputation with, that very rare thing, a single-vineyard cognac, sold to and by such considerable caravanserais as Lasserre and Maxim's in Paris, the Pyramide at Vienne and L'Oustau de Baumanière at Baux, and pretty well every other three-starred, and many a two-starred, establishment in Michelin.

But even he finds it best to sell half of each year's output of cognac to the big firms, after three years' ageing, to finance his further ageing of the rest, and he is frank in his gratitude to such houses: they pay for the publicity that made cognac famous, and that keeps its name in the public's mind. Without them, he says, cognac itself would be forgotten—and as for Marcel Ragnaud's Grande Champagne. . . ! The big firms pay for a great deal of research and development, too, from which eventually the whole trade benefits.

This, indeed, is where armagnac is at a disadvantage with cognac: whatever the relative merits of these two great brandies, one reason why armagnac is so much less well-known in the world at large is that there are no Martells or Hennessys, Rèmy-Martins or Bisquit-Dubouchés or Courvoisiers, in Armagnac, to make the product famous by their advertising, not only to their own benefit, but to that of their smaller rivals, who cannot afford to advertise at all.[2]

*   *   *

Some of the shippers have vineyards. Martell have probably the most, but their vines can produce only twenty per cent of the firm's yearly requirement of brandy for blending; Hennessy's vineyards produce only about ten per cent of theirs.

Bisquit-Dubouché have planted eight hundred acres of their

---

[2] Many who are qualified to judge—and I quote the November 1971 issue of the 'Nouveau Guide' of MM. Henri Gault and Christian Millau as an example—maintain, too, that many of the best-known commercial houses of Armagnac, besides being far less able financially than those of Cognac to sustain expensive and intensive advertising campaigns, are less jealous of the reputation of their product.

twelve-hundred-acre property in the Fins Bois region with vines, which produce about thirty per cent of their total requirements— but these are not so considerable as Martell's or Hennessy's, and in any case they need wines from the Grande and Petite Champagnes for their blends.

Salignac and Rémy-Martin are two sizeable firms each of whose vineyards can produce only a token amount of brandy in relation to the firm's needs.

Other great firms, though, have neither vineyards nor stills: the outstanding example is Courvoisier, whose output is comparable to those of Martell and Hennessy. (The three firms between them are responsible for half the total trade in cognac, pretty well equally divided.)

Their function, such a firm as Courvoisier will say, is not to grow wine, or to distil it into brandy, but to buy immature brandies and age and blend them: to buy skilfully and blend skilfully. This attitude—similar to that of such champagne houses as Krug, who own no vineyards—is shared by smaller firms of such distinction as Otard, Prunier, Delamain, Denis-Mounié, and Hine.

And this is what all the great firms do, and it is by far their most important function, whether they own vineyards or not, whether they distil brandy or not—they buy, age and blend.

*   *   *

The distiller, whether *bouilleur de cru* or big firm, must complete his distillation by 31 March, for the age of a cognac starts at 1 April: if brandy is not a finished product by then, it will not be regarded officially as a year old until the following 31 March— when money could have been tied up in it for all but two years.

After that comes the tasting of samples. At firms like Martell and Hennessy, samples from their own vineyards and distilleries, as well as from brokers and from *bouilleurs de cru*; at other firms, from *bouilleurs* and brokers only.

Even Hennessy, with vineyards of their own, buy each year from 2,500 different sources, and Maurice Fillioux, the firm's famous *maître de chai*, which is to say, in a cognac house, the taster-in-chief (as well as the one reponsible for buying, maturing, blending, and much else), keeps a card-index of every sample ever tasted, whether it was accepted or rejected and, in either case, why.

In Monsieur Fillioux's room I picked cards at random and read that this sample had been turned down because the distilling must have been begun with too much of the lees in the cask of wine; that one because it had come from a *cuvier* that had been kept only half-full for too long, and showed traces of oxidization.

A qualified chemist acts as liaison between Monsieur Fillioux and the distillers, explaining what has gone wrong and how—if they want—they can get it right next time.

Monsieur Fillioux, who looks like one of the younger television dons, represents the sixth generation of his family in the direct male line to be *maître de chai* at Hennessy. He is a bachelor himself, but while I was in Cognac in November 1971 his nephew Yann Fillioux, himself a taster, got married, so there is a chance not only of a seventh but of an eighth generation of les Fillioux. Meanwhile, the present one works in a room reigned over jointly by an oil painting of his father and a bas-relief portrait in terra cotta of his grandfather.

By an agreeable coincidence, Martell's *maître de chai*, François Chapeau, now just over sixty, who began with the firm in 1930 under his father and uncle, is also the sixth generation of the same family in the direct male line to serve his firm. He is older than Monsieur Fillioux, and to look at might be a discreet family solicitor, with (appropriately) a nose that looks as sensitive as the late Ernest Thesiger's. The two great men speak of each other with enormous respect, as a Hobbs might speak of a Grace, save that they are even more interesting, as being contemporaries. Perhaps I should say, as an Olivier of a Gielgud.

Monsieur Chapeau has told me how in tasting samples, whether from Martell's own vineyards and distilleries, from brokers or *bouilleurs de cru* he looks first to see if in the first place the wine had been right—the grape picked at the proper ripeness, fermentation correct; then if there had been carelessness in the distillery in separating heads and tails from heart at precisely the right moment; if temperatures had been wrong or the flow from the condenser too slow or too fast; whether there was any smack of oiliness, or hint of scorching in the spirit. He claims, quite incidentally and modestly, in the course of conversation, to be able to tell by the taste of a young cognac if there is something wrong in the very shape of a still.

In smaller, family firms, such as Denis-Mounié, Hine and Delamain, it is the partners themselves who taste, but with the same sort of inherited skill that Maurice Fillioux and François Chapeau can bring to bear—at Hine, for instance, it is Robert, Bernard and Jacques Hine, father, son and nephew; at Denis-Mounié, the cousins, Richard and Jacques Roullet; at Delamain, Alain Braastad-Delamain and Noël Sauzey, whose mother and whose mother-in-law respectively were Delamains. At Augier, the *maître de chai* comes from a longer direct line of tasters even than those at Martell and Hennessy: he represents the seventh generation of his family to serve the firm.

They told me at all these firms how they and their fathers and grandfathers before them had dealt with the same growers and distillers and their forebears, too, for generations: a *bouilleur de cru* knows a house 'style', knows how to distil and how to age cognac to that particular house's requirements, and knows that so long as he treads the same path there is always a buyer for his brandies.

Some of the grower-distiller families, for instance, who deal with Delamain have been doing so for two hundred years: they know that Delamain specialize in blending and shipping cognacs that are light in colour, dry and delicate in flavour (the firm's most famous quality is their 'Pale and Dry'), and they produce their brandies to suit.

For it must be remembered that the small distillers and grower-distillers do not sell all the year's distillation at once: they sell enough to cover expenses and the cost of living for a year, putting the rest away as an investment. So all distillers, small as well as great, have stocks of cognac of different years, a cask or casks of which they sell when they need more money or more room.

So there is always, somewhere in the region, a cask of the particular age that any shipper might want for a blend, and every shipper knows the distiller most likely to have the age or the style he wants, and if he is shrewd, and keeps his ear to the ground, knows too when he is most likely to get it.

Count Burignot de Varenne of the house of Augier smiles as he tells how, if you are a small family shipper, keen on getting fine old brandies for your blends, you must not only know but be on dropping-in terms with all the grower-distillers in the better regions, and their families, so that when you hear that the old man is poorly you go round with some bedside presents as an old friend. You go round yourself, of course; you do not send your agent or your broker, or even your wife or your son—so that you are not an unexpected visitor when it is a matter not of the sick-bed but of the death-bed, and are welcome indeed at the last melancholy rites, when you may well be given the opportunity, before you have even asked, to buy a cask or more of old cognac to help to pay for the funeral and meet the death duties. Or, more cheerfully, there might be a marriageable daughter, for whom a dowry must be found. . . .

*   *   *

Just as the method of distillation is the same in principle, whether carried out in the vast new distilleries of the most famous shippers or in the one still of a grower-distiller, so too the principle of ageing remains the same.

Edward Hyams has shown[3] that although the wine-growers and the vintners of the ancient Mediterranean and Near-Eastern worlds knew well how to make wooden casks, they long continued to use earthen amphorae, sealed with oil or with wax, for the storage of their wine. It was when wine-growing reached the more temperate regions of the north, where timber is harder and the climate moister, so that it does not dry out to brittleness in the summer, that wooden casks came into their own.

The adoption of wood for storage altered the techniques of vinification. Wood is porous to air in a way that earthenware is not—Mr Hyams here disagrees with the late Warner Allen[4]— and wine aged in wood differs from wine aged in earthenware.

The wine-growers of the Charentes would always have used

[3] Hyams, *Dionysus*, London and New York, 1965.
[4] Warner Allen, *A History of Wine*, London, 1961.

wood—the wood of the local forests—and when they began to make brandy, then that too would be stored in the wood of the region.

Brandy would sometimes have to be kept for many months, until there was a Dutch merchant around to sell it to; sometimes, there would be a surplus, more than a merchant wanted at the time, and brandy would have to be kept for a year or so. Kept in wood—local wood.

So it cannot have been long after the introduction of distilling to this part of France that it was known how storage in wood changed and improved the fiery young spirit—how the colourless liquid slowly took on a pale golden colour as well as tannin and a faint, sweetish flavour from the wood which, being porous to the air, allowed a gradual oxidization that at the same time was mellowing and softening it.

Pretty well all the colour and a good deal of the taste of cognac as we now know it comes from the wood in which it is aged— once upon a time it was all the colour—and the long experience that began some four centuries ago has made it certain what the wood must be. Just as it has in Armagnac, where the local black oak, seamed with black veins and mottled with black knots, brings on the local brandy more quickly than cognac, and gives it its dark colour and some, at any rate, of its earthy flavour.

Not that there is any law laid down as to what wood cognac must be aged in, whereas there is as to what vines may be grown, and in what zones; what methods of pruning and training; what kind of still and method of distillation; what may be added to the finished product, and in what quantity.

No. Although the law requires a minimum period of maturation in cask, it is not the law, but experiment, long experience, and the custom of the trade, that insist that cognac shall age in oak: not any oak, but French oak, and not any French oak, but oak only from the scattered woods of the Limousin or the great national forest of Tronçais.

And it is pertinent here to observe how much more completely French is cognac, compared with the Scottishness of Scotch whisky, for all its pipers and its plaids, its sporrans and its skean dhus, in the advertisements in the American magazines.

Cognac is distilled in France out of wine from French grapes and matured in French oak: the grain whisky that makes up at least half of any well-advertised Scotch is distilled in Scotland, it is true, but from imported maize (probably Romanian) and matured, with its blend of malt distilled from Scottish, English, Australian, South African or Indian barley, in casks of white American oak that has come from Arkansas either direct or by way of Spain.[5]

In relatively recent years, perhaps as oak from nearby forests of the Limousin became less plentiful and more expensive, the Cognaçais have tried Austrian oak, recommended to them, possibly, by the Bordelais, who have found it admirable for claret. But the colourless young cognac took on an unbecoming colour from a timber that does no harm to the red wines of Bordeaux. American oak, which does well by whisky, as we have seen, apparently gave cognac the wrong smell, and oak from Odessa, with its thick, spongy white 'veins' gave both a wrong colour and a wrong smell.[6] Monsieur Jean Taransaud, head of a privately-owned coopering firm, the biggest in Cognac, that has been handed on from father to son since 1755, did not know that there was any such thing as English oak. . . .

The only alternative to Limousin oak is from not much farther away—from the Tronçais forest in the very middle of France, barely a couple of hundred miles to the north-east, measured from Cognac, the heart of the cognac region, to the heart of the forest itself, which covers virtually forty square and unbroken miles.

It seems highly probable that until quite recent times only Limousin oak was used. The oak woods are scattered around the city of Limoges, only sixty or seventy miles from Angoulême, whence timber could go by road or downstream by the Charente to Jarnac and Cognac.

As recently as 1935 Robert Delamain wrote[7] of Limousin oak as being the only one used for the ageing of cognac, and of how

[5] For whisky casks, see Daiches, *Scotch Whisky*, London, 1969, and New York, 1970. For the provenance of barley used for malt whiskies, see McDowall, *The Whiskies of Scotland*, 1967, and New York, 1970.

[6] Brunet, *Manuel de Tonnellerie*, Paris, 1948.

[7] Delamain, *Histoire du Cognac*, Paris, 1935.

superior it was to the even more accessible timber of Aunis and Saintonge.

Since those days, a heavy toll has been laid upon the forests of Limousin, and there cannot be anything like enough oak in Aunis and Saintonge, even were it suitable, to meet the enormously growing demand from Cognac.

Meanwhile, however, better roads and bigger vehicles have augmented rail communications with Montluçon and the wood-cutters of the Tronçais and, as the timber of Tronçais is as suitable as that of the Limousin for the ageing of cognac, the two regions share the trade more or less equally.

To say that the oak from the one region and that from the other are equally suitable is not to say that they are precisely similar either in their own characteristics or in those with which they endow the spirit that is matured in them.

Two main kinds of oak grow in these French forests: the *chêne blanc* or *chêne pedonculé*, which is the commonest (its acorn hangs from a stalk), and the *chêne rouvre*, the acorn of which has no stalk, but grows direct from the branch. The other types of French oak—*noir* and *vert*—are rare in these parts.

In the smallish woods and forests of the Limousin these oaks, mixed with other trees, grow fifty metres or so apart, and are thick and sturdy; they increase in girth at the rate of two centimetres or so a year. In the Tronçais, which is almost all oak, they are closer together, and must grow tall to reach light and air. They put on girth at only about two millimetres annually.

The Tronçais forest is a place to visit; indeed it is given two stars ('*mérite un détour*') under the entry for St-Bonnet-Tronçais in the red Guide Michelin, and then another two-starred entry all to itself, under Tronçais simply, without benefit of hotel or restaurant. (I have eaten simply but very well at the modest Hôtel du Commerce at Cérilly, on the edge of the forest: one goes from bar to restaurant through the kitchen, and sees with what care the chicken is cooked in white wine—to precede the pork chops, if there is no fish that day—and how good the butter that is beaten into the mashed potatoes.)

The trees of the Tronçais seem so tall and slender to an Englishman that he can hardly believe them to be oaks. Many of its oldest and tallest trees are signposted and named (what was once the Chêne de Pétain is now the Chêne du Maréchal), and I have seen trees there eighty and ninety feet high. The Chêne Jacques Chevalier, for instance, is about ninety-two feet high, but is a modest 14 feet round at four and a half feet above the ground.

It was the photograph of a Tronçais oak called Apollon, felled in 1953, that was widely reproduced for years as 'the most beautiful tree in France', so tall and graceful was it.

The Tronçais oak, therefore, has a closer grain than that of Limousin, is lighter and easier to work, but is a little more brittle. Both are a pale honey colour when cut, with the Tronçais showing sometimes a very slight pink tinge.

Throughout the cognac trade as a whole, the two woods are equally regarded—the very slightly higher cost of Tronçais reflects probably nothing more than the slightly higher transport costs. But this is not to say that each cooper or each distiller or each shipper likes the two woods equally.

Hennessy like Limousin; Martell like Tronçais. Both have cooperages of their own, in each of which a dozen or so *tonneliers*, coopers—the aristocracy of Cognac labour—perform the daily miracle of creating watertight casks without using glue or nails. Denis-Mounié, who have a three-man cooperage not for making but only for repairing casks, use only Limousin staves seasoned in their own yard.

At Bisquit-Dubouché, the *maître de chai* says firmly that 'wood is the secret of good cognac', and plays safe: at their cooperage, they make their casks half of Tronçais, half of Limousin. Courvoisier, which have no cooperage, buy casks for ageing of Limousin, and bigger blending vats of Tronçais.

I asked everyone in Cognac and Jarnac, and came to the conclusion that there is nothing really to choose: because of its wider grain, Limousin has more tannin, but imparts it to the brandy more slowly, so it is all the same in the long run.

Some say that, nevertheless, in the shorter runs, such as in the brandies of three-star and VSOP age and quality, they detect that Martell is rather the drier, Hennessy rather the sweeter, partly at any rate because Martell mature in Tronçais, which yields its tannin more quickly, Hennessy in Limousin. The difference between the two houses narrows in the older qualities. This confirms the general impression one is given of the difference between the two oaks.

Indeed, Robert Hine, who is a justly famous taster, said that he doubted very much whether he could tell the difference between a completed cognac that had been aged in Limousin and one aged in Tronçais, and Delamain, jealous of their particular style, are concerned only that the brandies they buy shall be pale in colour and light in character, leaving it to the distillers and distiller-growers they buy from to decide in what kind of wood this will be achieved.

It would seem that it is coopers rather than blenders that have preferences: it is noticeable that on the whole shippers with cooperages, such as Martell and Hennessy, make a positive choice, and that shippers without, such as Hine and Delamain, do not mind or, like Courvoisier, play safe. And what decides the cooper, I am sure, is what he is used to: it seems to be not a matter of taste in any literal sense.

Whichever region it comes from, the best oak-tree for a brandy cask is anything from about seventy to a hundred and fifty years old; the only part of use is the *fût*[8]—the trunk from just above the roots to the lowest branches, some nine or ten feet of clean, straight timber, easily sawn into staves. The rest goes along with timber from younger trees for railway-sleepers, for coffins—for all sorts of use less noble than the ageing of cognac.

The staves are seasoned in stacks, raised from the ground, and with air-space between each two staves, so that wind, rain and sun can season them, over a period of four to six years, to the characteristic silvery grey of the timber ready for fashioning into the 300-litre (66-gallon) ageing cask that is becoming more or less standard in the region, and costs some 350 francs, or into such enormous blending vats as the two I saw being made at the Taransaud *tonnellerie* for Prunier, each of them almost ten feet high, each holding more than three hundred gallons, the two of

[8] The French word for the trunk of a tree is the same as that for a wine-cask, though a cognac-cask is called a *barrique* and the big blending vat a *tonneau*.

them made by hand, without glue or nails, by seven men in five days.

The stacks of weathering staves are a frequent sight throughout not only the cognac region but also around Limousin and on the fringes of the Tronçais forest: stacks must be scattered to lessen the risk of fire.

Trees are felled in the winter, when the sap is down: the Office National des Forêts puts notices up at the Hôtel de la Ville announcing sales of cut wood at various points in the region between the end of September and mid-December.

De-afforestation has been a problem in the Limousin, where few of the scattered woods are state-owned, and where peasant proprietors have been reckless in cutting down oaks and re-planting with softwoods. It is different in the Tronçais, which is a *forêt domaniale*, strictly controlled, with a police force of forest rangers, and schemes both for marking trees that may be cut down and for replanting. There is now stricter control in the Limousin as well.

Each region, of course, is convinced that its oak is better than the other's. Each region is particularly proud that its best oak goes to Cognac, though there was a touch of typically French parochial patroitism in Monsieur Nicaud, the timber-factor of Limoges, who told me with great pride that as much as ten per cent of his output went to Cognac—timber on average more than a hundred years old, some of it two hundred, beautifully straight-grained, free of faults and knots—and then added, thoughtfully, of those customers of his, every inch of a hundred miles away, 'Mind you, it must be very boring for people in that dull country, the Charentes, not to have forests and lakes like we have, here in the Limousin.'

7. 'The Angels' Share'

ONCE the spirit is in wood, remarkable changes begin to take place, caused by interaction between the wood, the spirit and the outside air.

The raw, new, colourless brandy begins to draw into itself tannin, colour and taste—a sort of sweetness—from the inner surface of the cask, while at the same time, through the pores of the wood, the outside air is oxidizing the spirit.

With this air comes in, too, a certain amount of atmospheric humidity, exchanging itself, as it were, for the amount of alcohol that evaporates through the pores—at an average rate in Cognac (it may well be different elsewhere) of some three per cent a year. Some, indeed, say five per cent, and the French taxation authorities allow for six.

This loss of spirit through evaporation, referred to by lady journalists and advertisement copywriters as 'the angels' share', is said by Martell, for instance, to mean a loss to them of two million bottles a year; Hennessy's and Courvoisier's figures would be much the same.

Others put it at anything from 25,000 bottles a day to more than 12 million bottles a year, which works out at rather more—in any case, something like France's total consumption of cognac.

What this evaporation also does is cause and encourage the fungoid growth that turns the tiles of Cognac black.

The loss of volume and of strength varies according to climate. In a dry place there will be more loss of volume, less of strength; in a damp place, more strength will be lost, and less volume. This is important, because although cognac may be distilled only in the delimited Cognac area, it may be matured anywhere. It will be seen later how differently cognac matures in Britain—in London or Bristol, or Edinburgh—from in France.

New brandy is put into new wood. A newly-made cask would offer changes too violent to brandy that was already mellowing and acquiring colour, so it is broken in, as it were, by the brash new spirit, which the brash new wood breaks in, in its turn.

Henri Exshaw (who is unusual in maturing and blending his firm's very good cognacs not in the Charentes at all, but in Bordeaux, but whose practice in this matter of new wood for new brandy is typical of all the cognac firms) told me that his brand-new casks are used only for newly-distilled brandy, and only the new Fins Bois at that, not even the newest Petite or Grande Champagne.

After a year, the Fins Bois is racked (taken off any deposit it may have thrown) into older casks, and the now year-old cask, mellowed by the Fins Bois, is used for the new Petite Champagne, which again is racked into a still older cask after a year, and only then is the two-year-old cask used for the newest Grande Champagne.

Even so (and now I can take up the tale from another firm, for it was the Hines who first told me this, and again it is standard practice throughout the trade) the cognac is carefully and regularly tasted, and if it is found to be taking up too much tannin from the wood, and acquiring too soon the 'woody' taste that in general is to be avoided, then it is transferred from this two-year-old cask to an older one.

Obviously, the more the cask has been used the less colour and tannin it has to impart to the new brandy put into it, though age seems to have little effect on the porosity of the wood to the outside air. So cognac will age at much the same rate in an old cask as in a new one, losing alcohol and becoming gently oxidized but will take on less woodiness of flavour, less of the 'firmness' and staying-power given by the tannin, and less colour.

This is how such a firm as Delamain, for instance, succeeds in producing the old, but pale and lightly-flavoured brandies in which it specializes.

This is one of the many distinguished firms that do no distilling themselves, but age and blend what they buy from grower-distillers, many of whom have been supplying the same firms for generations, and know their house style. In any case, the house style of every firm of any standing is well-known throughout the region.

Delamain ask their farmers always to mature their brandies in old casks from the beginning, and then, having bought the pale brandies thus matured, and blended them, give them what little further ageing they think necessary after blending—usually only a year or two—in their own very big, very old, maturing vats.

Size as well as age is a factor—obviously, the bigger the maturing vat, the less wood to the gallon of brandy. And Delamain's vats are not only impressively big but impressively old: they date from before the phylloxera plague of 1878.

Whether or not a firm does its own distilling, as, among the big houses, Martell, Hennessy, Bisquit-Dubouché and Rémy-Martin for instance do, and Courvoisier for instance do not, and as none does of the smaller firms I have just mentioned—however the firm is organized, the style of its cognac, and the reputation of the house, depend on the *maître de chai* (or cellar-master, or chief taster).

It is he who tastes the newly-distilled brandies from his firm's own distilleries or from outside; he who decides what wood to put them into or to transfer them from.

Above all, he blends.

He will decide how much Fins Bois or Borderies is needed to give mellowness and body to his Grande and his Petite Champagne brandies, and how old each of the elements in the blend needs to be, and from which cask.

Even in such a firm as Rémy-Martin, specializing in a Fine Champagne, the taster has to decide what amount more than the fifty per cent of Grande Champagne that the law demands must be blended with the Petite Champagne, and from which casks, which grower, and which parts of the two zones he must draw his brandies.

French law does not permit the sale of brandy less than a year old, but as Britain, its best customer for cognac, along with many other importing countries, insists on three years for all spirits, the standard, or three-star, commercial cognac are all three years old or more.

But to produce a consistent blend, true to the style of a house, it is not enough—it is far from enough—simply to bottle all the three-year-old brandy in the place.

Some must be set aside to age for longer, some for a great deal longer, for the sake of the firm's more expensive blends—the VSOPs, the Extras, and the very old blends in very fancy bottles, with very grand names.

And the house style must be maintained by blending.

At Hennessy, for example, Maurice Fillioux makes a 'pattern' blend every two months of up to a score of different three-year-old brandies from different parts of the Grande Champagne, the Petite Champagne, the Borderies and the Fins Bois, some from the firm's own vineyards, some from grower-distillers, some from professional distillers, some from co-operatives.

Hennessy's Bras Armé, the brand-name now given to its standard three-star cognac, is constantly being blended to this pattern—every couple of months—samples from which Monsieur Fillioux tastes daily against his master-blend, just as every day he tastes the comparable quality of each of Hennessy's major competitors.

The pattern and the commercial output have to be blended anew every two months because of the constant variations in style of the brandies available.

Vintages as such do not make a great deal of difference once wine has been distilled into brandy, but they make enough, and so do variations in the way that casks are behaving, and variations in weather, to require constant vigilance if a branded cognac is to maintain consistency of character.

Sometimes a little more delicacy is needed—a hint more Grande or Petite Champagne. Sometimes there is a slight lack of bouquet—more Borderies. Perhaps the blend seems a little immature? More of the Fins Bois is added: it ages more quickly than the others.

The law permits three other means of maintaining consistency.

Apart from the distilled water that has to be added to the younger blends to bring them down to acceptable strengths (70 degrees proof on the Sykes scale for the British market, which is the same as the French 40, Gay-Lussac, and the American 80), the law permits the addition of cane-sugar, of caramel, and of an infusion of oak-chips.

The sugar is to soften the asperities still to be found in young or youngish brandies; it may be added directly, or it may be added in the form of a syrup, dissolved in brandy, but in this case the brandy in which it is dissolved must itself be entitled to the appellation 'cognac'. The amount added is limited by law to two per cent by volume.

So is the amount of caramel, which is burnt sugar. This is not to sweeten the blend—I am told that it is tasteless—but to deepen the colour of a commercial blend, and then keep it consistent, year after year. Although there is a fashion in some quarters for lighter and drier brandies (and rums and whiskies) this is not widespread. On the whole, brandy-consumers take a deep colour to mean age and quality—or so the shippers believe. In any case, they expect their favourite brand to be always the same shade, whenever and wherever they drink it: caramel ensures this. The amount of caramel used is also restricted by law: again some two per cent by volume.

There is no restriction on the amount of *le boisé*, the infusion of oak-chips. As François Chapeau, the Martell *maître de chai*, told me, *le boisé* limits itself. It is meant to give the effects of extra age to a blend, the argument being that if it is contact with the wood of the cask that mellows a brandy, then the addition of an in-fusion of the same sort of wood will hasten the process.

But it is not only contact with wood that matures a brandy: it is the breathing through the pores of the wood—breathing alcohol out and oxygen in.

So although the addition of an infusion of oak-chips will give the colour and the tannin, it will not give the softness, and this is why it must be used sparingly. Too much will merely make the brandy darker and woodier, which is what happens to brandies left too long in cask, but without the true mellowness of age.

Which is why the great tasters and the other experts in Cognac either turn up their noses, or laugh, or shrug their shoulders, or say pooh! or go through all these performances at once when you ask them about the fancy-shaped bottles you can buy in the town, each with a rough wooden carving inside—not a ship in a bottle, but some such figure as an angler or a man with a dog, cut out of pale new oak. The idea is that you take the brandy you have just distilled, or the cheap bottle you have just bought in the supermarket, and pour it into the fancy bottle, where it will acquire colour and the quality of age from the pale new oaken angler or man with gun-dog, inside.

'No control', say the experts: *le boisé* has to be used with care, discretion and a sparing hand, and it has to be an infusion, not simply raw wood, as in the bottles in the souvenir shops.

There is no secret about *le boisé*: the legitimacy of the practice is referred to in such standard works on cognac as that of R. Lafon, J. Lafon and P. Couillaud and in Mademoiselle Landrau's summary of the law relating to cognac (see Bibliographical Note).

But the trade does not go out of its way to bring it to one's attention: there is no mention of it in any of the beautifully produced books and booklets put out by the grander firms, and no distiller of my acquaintance has ever referred to it until I brought the matter up. No chapter on cognac in any nineteenth- or twentieth-century English book on wines and spirits mentions it, which suggests that it was never mentioned to any of their authors.

'Everyone does it,' said François Chapeau of Martell, when he explained how self-limiting the practice must necessarily be. They said the same at Denis-Mounié, pointing out that whilst the infusion gives an agreeable suggestion of greater age to the 'nose' of a cognac, quite a small amount makes it harsh and bitter on the tongue.

Yet some of the smaller firms claim not only to eschew the practice themselves, which is understandable, especially if they go in for paler cognacs, but never to have heard of it, which seems unlikely.

As long ago as 1757 Cooper's *The Complete Distiller*, based partly on De Jean's *Traité Raisonné de la Distillation*, published three years earlier in Paris, had this to say on how to imitate French brandy. First, one distilled an 'oil of wine' from dried lees, and with it flavoured a rectified spirit; then, it was a matter of softness and of colour:

'. . . the softness may in a great measure be obtained by distilling and rectifying the spirit with a gentle fire; and what is wanting of this criterion in the liquor, when first made, will be supplied by time; for it must be remembered, that it is time alone that gives this property to *French* brandies; they being at first, like our spirits, acrid, foul and fiery. But with regard to the colour a particular method is necessary to imitate it to perfection. . . .

'. . . French brandy that has acquired by age a great degree of softness and ripeness, is observed, at the same time, to have acquired a yellowish brown colour; and hence our Distillers have endeavoured to imitate this colour in such spirits as are intended to pass for *French* brandy. . . .

'. . . This being undeniably the case, let us try if we cannot discover this mighty secret; the ingredient from whence the *French* brandy acquires its colour.

'We have already observed that this colour is only found in such brandies as have acquired a mellow ripeness by age; it is therefore not given it by the Distiller, but has gained it by lying long in the cask. Consequently, the ingredient from whence this colour is extracted, is no other than the wood of the cask, and the brandy in reality is become a dilute tincture of oak.

'Since, therefore, the colour of *French* brandies is acquired from the oak of the cask, it is no difficulty to imitate it to perfection. A small quantity of the extract of oak, or the shavings of that wood properly digested, will furnish us with a tincture capable of giving the spirit any degree of colour required. But it must be remembered, that as the tincture is extracted from the cask by brandy, that is alcohol and water, it is necessary to use both in extracting the tincture; for each of these menstruums dissolves different parts of the wood. Let, therefore, a sufficient quantity of oak shavings be digested in strong spirit of wine; and also at the same time other oak shavings be digested in water: and when the liquors have acquired a strong tincture from the oak, let both be poured off from the shavings, into different vessels, and both placed over a gentle fire till reduced to the consistency of treacle.'

The author then goes on to explain how this tincture can be kept ready for use as required, and augmented and assisted by common treacle and by brown sugar.

It is not clear whether this use of tincture of oak shavings is taken, as are other chapters, from the French book, but it must be assumed that if this method was known to the mid-eighteenth-century English imitators of French brandies (cognac itself is specified, along with others) it must have been known, too, to the French distillers of the product imitated.

In which case, it has been in men's minds and memories a long time for any distiller or blender of cognac today to say that he has never heard of it.

8. '. . . And Such Great Names As These'

THE War of the Spanish Succession, 1701–13, disrupted the export trade in cognac, and especially the trade with England, just as it had become established with, as we noted in chapter 3, a newly created élite that was beginning to appreciate the different qualities of brandy—of brandies, that is, from various sources.

What these first connoisseurs were just beginning to learn before the war was the superiority of cognac over other brandies. The war itself, an ill wind blowing good, made it possible for their sons to learn how much better cognac could be even than the cognac their fathers had known.

While their best customers were marching with Marlborough to the Danube, or sat in their country houses, drinking the port secured to them by the Methuen Treaty and Sir Cloudesley Shovell's command of the seas,[1] the grower-distillers of the

---

[1] The Methuen Treaty, 1703, a result of the negotiations that brought Portugal from the side of Louis XIV into the Grand Alliance, provided that in return for the admission of British woollens to Portugal, Portuguese wines should continue to enjoy the one-third preference they had over those of France. It never caused the Whig, Hanoverian port completely to displace the Tory, Jacobite claret, but it established it as an after-dinner drink, when good cognac was still a relative newcomer.

Charentes had to put their brandies away in casks, made of their local oak, to wait for better times.

It was some consolation to discover how, as the cognac aged, it took on colour from the cask, mellowness and flavour. It was the birth of a new sort of cognac.

The birth, too, of a new sort of cognac trade. Some of the small farmers could not afford to hang on to their casks indefinitely: they had to sell for cash. Merchants moved in, buying cognac as a speculation, to put away against more peaceful times or, at any rate, against better prices. It was the beginning of cognac as big business, for the foundations were being laid on which some of today's greatest firms could begin building as soon as the war was ended. There is significance in Martell's having been founded in 1715, only two years after the signing of the Treaty of Utrecht. Firms such as Augier, founded in 1643, the oldest in the trade with an unbroken history,[2] had begun as brokers, now found themselves with stocks on their hands that they had been used to selling to shippers almost as soon as they had been bought.

Once big stocks came into existence, and the trade ceased to be a matter simply of each small farmer's cask or so of newly-distilled spirit being passed quickly on by middlemen to an export house in Rochefort or La Rochelle, it was Cognac that became important, because it was where the brokers gathered to be near the best brandies. (An exception is the smallish firm of Rouyer-Guillet, founded in 1701, still at Saintes.)

The next step was both logical and easy. Big stocks waiting to be sold meant evaporation: one cask would have to be topped up with brandies from another cask. After a time, it would not be with brandies of the same age, or from the same farmer. Thus it was learned how blending, as well as simple ageing, could improve a cognac. The brokers, who had first become warehousemen, were now blenders.

It is interesting that the earliest reference we now know of the quality of cognac compared with other brandies dates from

[2] Gourry of Segonzac hang out a signboard at their farm stating that they were founded in 1619, but they were then, and are now, *bouilleurs du cru*, not *négociants* or shippers.

this very time: Jean Gervais, an officer of the Angoulême Presidial, a provincial Court of Justice, in an official memorandum of 1726 on the export of eaux-de-vie, reported that the eau-de-vie of Cognac was now reckoned '*la meilleure du monde*'. A pattern had been set.

*　　*　　*

Today, every firm, great and small, and every grower-distiller, puts away cognac not merely for ageing, but some of it for great ageing, as they all have been doing for a century and more.

Thus it is that while the cognac trade sells about a hundred million bottles a year, at home and abroad, there is always a reserve stock, maturing in its casks of Limousin or Tronçais oak, of the equivalent of four-and-a-half to five times as much—the better part of five hundred million bottles of cognac.

Not all of this, by a long chalk, is destined for great age. Some will be quite new brandy waiting the necessary three years to become part of a three-star blend; some will have only two more years, some only one, to fulfil the same destiny. Although French law requires only a minimum of a year's ageing before cognac can be put on the market, eighty per cent of cognac is for export, and many export markets—Great Britian, which is cognac's best customer, among them—demand three.[3] And, in this context the age of a brandy means the age of the youngest brandy in the blend. A cognac blended of seven-, five-, three-, and one-year-old brandies is a one-year-old brandy.

In many of the big firms something like eighty per cent of production is of three-star brandy. Even so, such firms are so big that the remaining twenty per cent of older brandies can run into hundreds and thousands of bottles.

Some of the smaller firms produce a much higher proportion of finer qualities, and one of the very big firms—Rémy-Martin, which disputes with Bisquit-Dubouché fourth place for output, some way after the big three of Hennessy, Martell and Courvoisier—produces no three-star at all, only VSOP quality and above.

[3] See Appendix III for latest analysis of export distribution.

Officially, the various qualities of cognac are a function of age, and the law lays down what these ages may be. This is all that the law can do, for with supervision there can be no dispute about age whereas opinions, as we shall see, may well differ, and differ widely, as to whether this blend is better than that, or that better than this.

There are six *'comptes'* or index figures in the code that controls the labelling and sale of cognac:

o signifies brandy certified as being of the year of distillation.
1 signifies brandy certified as being more than a year old.
2 signifies brandy certified as being more than two years old.
3 signifies brandy certified as being more than three years old.
4 signifies brandy certified as being more than four years old.
5 signifies brandy certified as being more than five years old.

There is much virtue in that 'certified as being'. Because of the considerable evaporation of brandy from the casks in which it matures, and because of the amount of topping-up that has to be done in consequence—far more than can possibly be thoroughly supervised, even by the hundred or so inspectors constantly at work in Cognac—from the French Excise, the Institut Nationale des Appellations d'Origine, the Ministry of Agriculture, the Repression des Fraudes, the Bureau National Interprofessionnel du Cognac, and who knows what other hawk-eyed organization —no official certificate is given that will entitle a brandy to call itself six years old or over. The highest claim that a brandy can make officially is that it is 'more than five years old'. It is like a horse's being described as 'aged' or 'beyond mark of mouth'.

The youngest cognac on sale in France has to be *compte no. 1*: more than one year old; in practice, it is generally regarded as being eighteen months.[4] If it is from a well-known house that exports to Britain it will, in fact, be *compte no. 3*: more than three years old.

It will almost certainly be described as three-star.

Hennessy are usually given the credit for the star system of designating cognacs. Once upon a time, the notion was that one

[4] Letter to *International Herald Tribune*, Paris, 22 January 1971, from M. Christian Braastad, Managing Director, Courvoisier.

star denoted a three-year-old brandy, two stars a four-year-old, and three stars five, but now it means simply a firm's standard, regular, youngest and cheapest blend—not a liqueur brandy.

One story is that a member of the Hennessy family got the idea of a star from an ornamental device on an office window-catch. Another is that the stars came into use after the great phylloxera blight: casks containing the first good vintage after production was well under way again were marked with a comet (after the legendary 'year of the comet'—1811—the wines of which were extraordinary), the second good vintage with two stars, and so on.

The mark is now so well-known, as designating the youngest and, therefore, the cheapest commercial brand of any well-known house, that Salignac, for instance, must consider it debased, for they mark with five stars what used to be their three-star brandy for the United Kingdom. Hennessy, its supposed originators, feeling much the same, or feeling at any rate that it is now insufficiently distinctive, have dropped stars altogether, and what used to be their own three-star brandy is now Bras-Armé, styled after the crest of the founding family.

The Hennessy move, which took place in 1962, followed Martell's decision, of about a year before, to replace their VSOP with 'Medallion'—a word which has the advertising and labelling advantage of looking virtually the same in French and in English. There is a tendency, though it is still, after more than ten years, a very gradual one, away from the stars and initials of a not very long tradition towards brand names, perhaps on the advice of marketing magicians and advertising wizards.

Let us not suppose, though, that a three-star brandy is simply any one batch of brandy that is three years old: it will be a blend, as we have seen, of brandies probably from at least four different zones—Grande Champagne, Petite Champagne, Borderies and Fins Bois—softened, coloured and mellowed by the addition of sugar, caramel and *le boisé*. With older brandies as rare as they are, and as expensive, it is most unlikely that it will contain any appreciable amount of older brandy than its obligatory three-year-old.

All the same, as very nearly ninety per cent of the 16 million or so bottles of cognac coming to the United Kingdom are three-star it is as well to remember that this is not cognac *inferior* to the other grades, but *younger*—and, therefore, much more likely to be darkened and mellowed by additives. But it still comes only from the area delimited by law, is made in the prescribed way, and its only additives are those permitted by law, to the extent that the law permits.

It is a measure of Britain's historic importance in the cognac trade that the initials VSOP, by which most, by far, of the shippers designate their next oldest quality—the quality universally recognized as that of a liqueur, after-dinner brandy—stand for the English words 'very superior old pale' (or 'very special old pal', as printed on the wine-list at Cognac's Restaurant l'Auberge —one knows the sort of chap they mean, precisely).

Rémy-Martin, who do not produce a three-star, but specialize in VSOP, not only took up the French jest that as cognac is a French product it ought to stand for *'versez sans oublier personne'*— 'pour it out without forgetting anyone'—but actually patented the phrase.

And Alec Waugh recalls having been told in Cognac that it ought to stand for *'vieux, sans opinion politique'*. I have never come across this explanation myself, and fear that it would be far from the truth. Sad though I am to say it, I believe cognac to be conservative.

A cognac bearing the designation 'VSOP' (or the less frequent 'VO 'or 'Réserve') must come under the umbrella of *compte no. 4*—must not include in its blend, that is, any brandy less than four years old: again, in practice, fifty-four months. It is from this point onwards that the great reserves of much older brandies become of enormous importance to a cognac house. More still when we come to *compte no. 5*—blends more than five years old— into which category come the brands bearing such honorifics as 'Extra', 'Extra Vieille', 'Vieille Réserve', even 'Trés Vieille Grande Réserve', 'Cordon Bleu', 'Cordon Argent', and 'Age Inconnu'.

Also into this category come brandies named not only after a Patriarche, but after Napoleon himself—the Great, so-called, not the Third—Louis Phillippe, our own Edward VII, Prince

5. Coopers at work in a great Cognac distillery

6. A *paradis* where fine old brandies age until they are used for blending; these cognacs are probably not more than 50–60

Hubert de Polignac, Princes de Cognac, and such great names as these. However exalted the rank, all that the law requires is that no brandy given such a style should be less than five years old: *Compte no. 5 . . . plus que cinq ans.* (The code gives as its examples, '*Les désignations "Extra", "Napoléon", "Vieille Réserve" et assimilées*'.)

Ah, Napoleon! To discuss how this particular great name comes to be so closely associated with cognac *mérite un detour*, which is undertaken in the next chapter. Suffice it here to say that by 1946 the French authorities had decided that there was nothing for it but to accept 'Napoléon' as signifying a cognac of some age, greater than that of VSOP: five years and over.

* * *

Although the law would permit a blend of, say, a four-year-old and a five-year-old brandy, or even an unblended four-year-old, to be sold as a VSOP, and a straight five-year-old or blend of five-year-old and six-year-old to be sold as a Napoléon, this is not the way a serious cognac house looks at it.

Every such house has its *paradis*—the 'paradise' that houses its oldest cognacs, some of which, it is true, are there as museum pieces, simply, but most to be drawn upon to give style and the more appealing qualities of age to their VSOPs and older blends.

Some, as at Martell and Hennessy, have been built up over the generations. These two great houses, friendly though their relations are with each other—and they are, indeed, very friendly —each claim to have the greatest stocks of old brandies in the world. There cannot be much difference between them.

Some of such considerably smaller but time-honoured and highly-regarded houses as Augier, Denis-Mounié, Hine and Delamain have also built up notable collections. I have drunk remarkable old unblended cognacs at Salignac and at Camus.

Other big houses, such as Courvoisier, have built up their fine reserves of old cognac by buying in large amounts, but shrewdly, over a relatively few recent years from grower-distillers. The forward-looking Union Coopérative des Viticulteurs Charentais (UNICOOP) has stocked a fine *paradis* from the reserves of its 4,500 members.

Some small houses keep their own stocks fairly modest, to minimize the amount of capital they would have to tie up, but always know which farmer to turn to when a specially distinguished cognac of great age is needed for a blend.

*   *   *

There is a deep religious hush, a dim religious light, about a *paradis*.

They take good care, the Cognaçais, not to disturb the cobwebs, or to clean the windows. (Cognac is almost entirely a place of *chais*—above-ground warehouses, like Spanish sherry bodegas—not of cellars.) It is a good combination of stage-management and public-relations practice to let the privileged visitor to a *paradis* feel that he treads upon holy ground.

Nor must I be so blasé as to pretend that I felt no sense of awe in the Martell *paradis*, for instance, where there is cognac of that most famous year, 1811 (a great year for cognac, as for claret), and of the year of Waterloo: the same sense of awe that prompted Winston Churchill, visiting Madeira after the war, and given a glass of a vintage—not a solera—Bual 1792, to cry out, 'D'you realize, gentlemen, that when this wine was made, *Marie Antoinette was still alive*?'

A sense of awe, too, in the tiny, immemorially dusty establishment of Noël Dor, who boasts that his Age d'Or is an unblended 1893, the same age as he is. After we had tasted the cognac of what to him was the year of Austerlitz and to me Trafalgar—one of six bottles left, and kept in wood until 1967: dark and heavy, but drinkable—he offered me a glass of his 1834 with the words, '*Louis Philippe est mort, mais pas ce cognac!*' [5]

It is just as impressive to dip into Hennessy's great bible—which seems not too noble a word for the directory of the contents of a famous *paradis*—and see the stately progression down page after page of, for instance, one cask of Monsieur Pelletant's 1800 Grande Champagne, nine demijohns (big, wicker-covered glass carboys, that is) and then another eight of the same grower's demijohns, probably bought in two separate

[5] The small firm of Dor, like those of Commandon, Gautier, and Favraud, now belongs to Bénédictine.

lots; then twenty-three other nineteenth-century vintages, from years of revolution and years of war, years of French empire, kingdom of the French and French republic, all the way down to the nineteen-thirties.

Each entry has its cryptic note, symbol and set of initials, revealing to the initiated when which generation of Fillioux tasted it; what he thought of it; when it was tasted last; what its alcoholic strength is; and what *coupe*, or blend, it has had a part in.

Many of these very old cognacs—in some firms' *paradis*, all—are kept in glass carboys or demijohns (*bonbonnes*) and not in wood. Indeed, Hennessy are unusual in having a whole cask of 1800 still in wood.

The reason for the glass demijohns is that although cognac improves in wood, it improves only for so long. The length of time varies, according to the original style of the brandy, the size and the age of the cask in which it is kept, the temperature and humidity of the *chai*, and other, more imponderable, factors. To some extent, brandy, like wine, is a living creature, in that it grows up, reaches maturity, and then old age. Different casks of cognac, like wines and different men and women, reach maturity and old age at different rates.

In the Denis-Mounié *paradis*, for instance, I tasted a 1918 and a 1929 Grande Champagne with Jacques Roullet, and we both found the 1918 smoother, less woody and astringent than the 1929—presumably, suggested Monsieur Roullet, because the 1918 in its youth had been taken sooner out of a cask of new or newish wood and into older wood. It is never in these cases a matter of vintage differences, which are pretty well completely rubbed out by distillation, and finally by maturation.

All the same, the 1929 had great body and bouquet—a very little 'would be a benefactor to a blend', said my guide. And at the same firm, tasting the younger brandies, we found a 1965 much darker in colour and woodier in flavour than a 1961, simply through its having been aged in newer wood.

At Salignac, another example of how different brandies can each give qualities of their own to a blend. Having found an 1865 and an 1893 too heavy to taste for pleasure, we tasted a 1914

Grande Champagne against a 1934. The first was prettier on the nose, the second pleasanter in the mouth. A good Salignac of premium quality will have a little of each.

*   *   *

Very roughly—very roughly indeed—the life-span of cognac in wood is the same as the human being's allotted span.

Most cognac houses, therefore, transfer their old brandies from wood to glass at fifty or, exceptionally, at up to seventy years old. Brandy does not develop at all in glass, whether the glass be *bonbonne* or bottle.

As Hugh Johnson once put it, 'there is an analogy in the writing of a story. While it is in the author's mind, it grows, changes, develops. Then he writes it. Read it a hundred years later; it is still the same story. The moment of bottling brandy is comparable to the moment of committing a story to paper.'

Some of the very old brandies, as I have said, are museum pieces, simply. I have tasted some of these veterans: it was like what I imagine sleeping with a very famous but old lady must be—academically interesting but unpleasurable. The old brandies can be coarse, astringent, woody—perhaps the old ladies, too.

The old, but not quite so old, brandies are blended as bases to be used, along with much younger brandies of the highest quality, for the great premium blends of each house.

Thus, at Hennessy there is a basic blend, *coupe no. 1*, first compounded by the father of Maurice Fillioux, the present *maître de chai*, of a whole range of brandies from the eighteen-sixties to the early nineteen-hundreds, with 1884 as the median date, and another *coupe*, called *Moyen 50*, with 1919 as its median date.

Much of the 1884 *coupe no. 1*, and a very little of the 1919 *Moyen 50*, is used as a base, completed with a blend of younger brandies from as late as the nineteen-twenties, for Hennessy's Extra, the firm's oldest and most expensive *marque*, twice the price, even, of the famous XO.

For this, the next oldest, still very expensive, blend the proportions are reversed—much of the 1919 base, a very little of the 1884, and completion by the addition of brandies about fifty years old and older.

It is much the same at Martell, where they told me that the average of their Cordon Argent, roughly the equivalent of the Hennessy XO, is some sixty years old; the Extra, comparable with Hennessy's, well over seventy. All the brandies in these two blends come from carboys, not casks.

One need hardly add that only very small amounts of brandies of this quality are blended each year—250 cases, or 3,000 bottles, of Martell Extra in 1971, for instance, for the millionaires of Zurich and Dusseldorf, Houston and New York, to say nothing of Tokyo, Paris and London—and that each year there are careful tastings to decide which of the next oldest brandies may be promoted to the *paradis* to take their as yet modest place in the premium blends, usually as they come up to about fifty years old.

The directors of both firms are frank about their preference in each case for the second rarest and most expensive of their blends—for the Martell Cordon Argent or the Hennessy XO rather than either firm's Extra.

Oh yes, they agree: they make very little of the Extra and with enormous care; it is made of the very oldest and most precious of the cognacs in the *paradis*; but to *their* taste—and I have had Michel Martell, senior partner in his family firm, say this to me, and also Alain de Pracomtal, the managing director of Hennessy —it is too heavy, too woody, too *fatigant*. A great brandy in each case, and they are proud to make it for the few connoisseurs who dote upon it—and who can afford it. But the Martell Cordon Argent, says Monsieur Martell; the XO, says Comte Alain de Pracomtal; is just that whisper lighter in the mouth, more elegant.

Yet again, it is the same at Bisquit-Dubouché, where the directors and the highly experienced and knowledgeable *maître de chai* are at one in preferring their Napoléon, which is a Fine Champagne of an average thirty years old, to the Extra Vieille, twenty years older, a Grande Fine Champagne, and a good deal rarer and dearer.

So, too, at the other end of the size-scale, with Marcel Ragnaud who makes his single-vineyard Grande Fine Champagne on his own property at Ambleville, and drinks his twenty-year-old Réserve Spéciale in preference to the thirty-five-year-old Grande Réserve Fontveille, which I agreed with him in finding heavy and woody, for all its superb bouquet.

It is very like being in Oporto, where one finds that shippers there with famous names, while immensely proud of the vintage ports that they send to Britain to be bought at high prices, and treated with profound respect, prefer themselves to drink and to offer their fine, delicate old tawnies. Their vintage ports, they say, are magnificent, but heavy and cloying.

The cousins Roullet at their family firm of Denis-Mounié drink the VSOP they blend for the United Kingdom in preference to their Grande Réserve Edward VII (so-named because theirs was the first house in Cognac to be granted a royal warrant by a British monarch—in 1908) and to their Extra Vieille.

Here, too, is an instance of the same quality being blended differently for the home and for the foreign market. The VSOP blend for France and that for the United Kingdom are precisely the same in quality and in average age, but paler brandies of the right age are picked out initially for the British market; they are kept in 'dry', which is to say older, wood before blending, and that only for a short time, and then blended in vat, not cask, so that there shall be less effect of the wood on the brandy.

It is curious that they will tell you at one cognac house that they darken their brandies with caramel only because of the consumer demand, by which they mean overseas, and particularly British, demand, for dark brandies—black, so to speak, is beautiful—and that others will say that nowadays the vogue is for the pale and dry: 'Pale and Dry' is, indeed, the name of Delamain's very fine better-than-VSOP blend, and pale and dry has been the house style for seventy years.

One must suppose that there are different tastes within the same market, but my own belief is that the general trend is flowing more strongly than some of the biggest houses realize towards the lighter brandies: it is no longer a matter of 'pale' on the label, as in VSOP, but dark in the bottle, just as the cynics say of sherry-drinkers, that they want 'dry' on the label, sweet in the bottle.

At Augier I was shown old labels of the firm's 'VSOB'—'Very Superior Old Brown'. Not only has this mark long disappeared, but the taste for what was inside the bottle to justify it is also disappearing.

It is hardly surprising. Between writing paragraphs of this very chapter, I was entertained to luncheon in his rooms in Albany by George Rainbird, until recently chairman of the International Wine and Food Society. After the two noble burgundies that had accompanied the roast partridges, he gave us with the coffee, 'as an experience', he said, a glass apiece of Ebenezer Bayley's Old Brown Brandy, discovered in the cellars of an old Yorkshire pub, whence it had been a speciality of the house some time before the eighteen-seventies. It looked like lung tonic, and tasted like marching-boots. I do not care to put down on paper any of our guesses as to the colouring element in the compound. We cleansed our palates with the Wine Society's excellently pale and delicate twenty-year-old cognac, for which I have never been so grateful.

I suspect that those who still maintain that the market demand is overwhelmingly for darker brandies are really seeking an excuse for the continued use of caramel, which makes it all the easier for them to keep their brandies consistent in colour.

* * *

There are different views in Cognac as to whether brandies should be aged before or after blending but the weight of opinion is in favour of ageing afterwards. Hervé de Jarnac, for instance, at Salignac, holds that blending, whether for three-star or for the more expensive brands, should be done before the components are even a year old, and Count Burignot de Varenne at Augier, where they age for at least twenty months after blending, enlarged upon this: one- or two-year-old cognacs blended and then aged for three years, he said, make a far better cognac than a blend of five-year-old bottled immediately after blending.

At Courvoisier, for their three-star, they blend after a year in cask and about two in vat; then age for between another year and two, again in vat. There is less oxidization in vats than in casks—ageing is slower but, they say, the blending is all the more uniform and complete.

Differences of opinion between various houses are sharper over the blending of brandies from the different zones.

We have seen that one major house, Rémy-Martin, one of the biggest after Martell, Hennessy and Courvoisier, makes no three-star cognac, only VSOP quality and above. Moreover, it produces only those cognacs that are entitled to be labelled 'Fine Champagne'—blended, that is, only of brandies from the Grande Champagne and Petite Champagne zones, with at least fifty per cent of the blend from the Grande Champagne.

Their submission, and they have made much of it in their publicity, is that as these are the zones that produce the finest and the most expensive brandies, therefore, a Fine Champagne is the best of all blends, and that blends that include brandies from other zones are, for that very reason, inferior.

Other firms make Fine Champagnes, too, but have not put forward such sweeping claims. Yet others dispute the claims altogether. The best cognac, they say, is a blend—not only of the very fine Grande and Petite Champagne brandies but, because these are not only delicate but slow to age, of brandies that will add the quality of age and others that will give backbone and bouquet.

It is much the same as the argument of the traditionalists in Champagne against the makers of *blanc de blancs*, who claim that as it is the white grapes that give delicacy and finesse to a champagne, then a wine made only from the juice of white grapes must necessarily be *all* delicacy and finesse.

Not at all, say the traditionalists, such as Monsieur Krug and Madame Bollinger, who will have no truck with such heresies. Champagne is a blend, and always has been, of black and white grapes, each of which has something to offer: the white grapes, finesse; the black grapes, body and fruit. *Blanc de blancs* may be delicious, but it is not a true, traditional champagne.[6]

Thus, the other great houses, who buy vast amounts of the Grande Champagne and Petite Champagne brandies (Martell, Hennessy and Courvoisier between them buy about seventy per

[6] See Ray, *Bollinger*, 1971, chapter 8.

cent of these two zones' total output), insist that the best way to use them is in smallish amounts to give breeding and elegance to their three-stars and the like, whilst blending them in the older *marques* with the Borderies and the Fins Bois that will give them character.

The Grande and Petite Champagne brandies, they say, mature too slowly to make good VSOPs unblended, unless the VSOPs were to be matured for uneconomically lengthy periods.

Even small firms that do in fact produce Fine Champagne and Grande Fine Champagne blends agree with this.

At Delamain, for instance, they tell you that while their 'Pale and Dry' is a Grande Fine Champagne, it is only possible to produce it satisfactorily by blending seven different Grande Champagne brandies of an average age of twenty years, which makes the blend necessarily expensive. They say that to produce a commerical VSOP in considerable quantities and at a competitive price, which means after only perhaps an average of some five years' maturing, they would have to use some Borderies and Fins Bois or the blend would seem immature and lacking in character.

Camus, who make three-star, VSOP and other qualities in the traditional way, also make two single-vineyard cognacs, one from a small property of their own, one from the Château d'Uffaut, in the Grande Champagne, which they manage for the owners, producing 50,000 bottles a year of its Grande Fine Champagne. This is supplied to crowned and other presumably discriminating (or, at any rate, publicity-worthy) heads and to smart Paris restaurants, but Philippe Camus himself, with whom I drank it at the Moulin de Cierzac restaurant, just outside Cognac, said of it that, delicate and *bouqueté* as it was, it needed the backbone of Borderies or Bois: compared with their commercial Napoléon or Célébration, it was 'incomplete'.

'You like it or you don't,' he said, using the same phrase about their racier and rarer (only 1,200 bottles a year) Château du Plessis, one hundred per cent Borderies, which is to be had at no less a temple of the belly than the Grande Véfour in the Palais Royal, and then, I gather, only by asking specially.

I have not tasted the Château du Plessis, which I gather is

more fragrant, less fine than the Château d'Uffaut. I think I might well prefer the Château d'Uffaut, for I like the lighter, more elegant brandies: I have already mentioned my predilection for the Delamain Pale and Dry, but this is of a greater average age than the VSOPs of commerce, and I can well believe that it is age in the slower-maturing Grandes and Petites Champagnes that makes them, to me, so acceptable—that when I drink a three-star or ordinary VSOP I should be grateful for the sturdier brandies that grow up more quickly.

One of the brandies, though, that I enjoyed most during my various periods of residence in Cognac was after a luncheon with the Roullet family—a Denis-Mounié Grande Champagne 1935, shipped to London by Justerini and Brooks in 1936 and bottled in 1969 at the natural strength it had then reached: a mere 61 degrees Sykes compared with the standard 70. Then it had been brought back to France. It had never known, I was told, sugar or caramel or *le boisé*: it had lost alcoholic strength by the very way it had been matured, and so had never needed dilution with distilled water. It was a miracle of dryness and delicacy, and so low in alcohol that there could not have been a headache in a hogshead.

But that 'very way it had been matured'—ah, that is the secret. . . .

Here was what is called 'early-landed' brandy—to be more precise, in this case, 'early-landed, late-bottled'. A brandy can be one or the other or, as in this case, both. Sometimes the two phrases are used indiscriminately, as being synonymous. Strictly, they are not so. A brandy can be 'early-landed' in England and then bottled no more 'late' than it might have been had it stayed in Cognac. Or it can be 'late-bottled' in France, having never been 'landed'—in Britain, that is—at all. In which case, it would not resemble a brandy that had been late-bottled in Britain.

This particular brandy was early-landed in that it had been shipped to London when only a year old, and late-bottled in having been matured in wood for well over thirty years, in a softer, damper climate than it would have known in its home town, before bottling. The pores in the wood of the cask breathed out alcohol and breathed in the soft, damp English air, and the result was a brandy quite different from any that had not left the shores of France until it was in bottle.

Such brandies are highly prized in Britain. Highly priced, too, for money has to be tied up in them while they are maturing. In France, they are considered flabby and mawkish, and the taste for them a typical English eccentricity. They would not mature to this style in Cognac, but it might well be that they would in Calais, say, or Quimper: the point is that no Frenchman would bother, and if such sophisticated Anglophiles as the Roullets want a few bottles in their cellars for their English friends, then they must buy them in Britain. (I have even brought back such bottles yet again to England—bottles bestowed upon me by the hospitable Hines—and had them waved through the Customs by a knowledgeable officer, who observed that they had already paid duty once: 'You don't really want to pay it again, do you?')

Just as a Cognaçais must go to London (or, perhaps, to Bristol or Edinburgh) for his early-landed, late-bottled brandy, so too for his vintage brandy. Since 1962 the rule is that the French authorities will not certify on the *acquit jaune*, the official yellow ticket ('*Certificat délivré pour des eaux-de-vie justifiant l'appellation d'origine controlée Cognac*') that must accompany every consignment of cognac, from still to salesman, any age greater than *compte no. 5*: more than five years old. After that age there has to be topping-up, and it is not possible to make sure that all topping-up of every brandy in every cellar is with brandy of the same age. So it has not been possible for this past dozen years in France to buy a bottle of cognac with a vintage year on the label—no label may claim what an *acquit jaune* does not bestow.

Abroad, though, it is another matter. A London shipper may land a cognac certified by *acquit jaune* as being, say, a 1971, for this is less than five years old; and keep it himself, not topping-up, as this would spoil the effect he is after, until he bottles it himself, knowing its age, any time from ten to fifty years later.

Thus, to take the current lists of a Bristol firm and of a big chain as examples, Harveys of Bristol list, among others:

Harvey's 1940 Petite Champagne landed 1964, bottled 1964. This is late-bottled, but not early-landed.

Frapin 1943 Grande Champagne landed 1963, bottled 1972.
An interesting one this—twenty years in wood in France and then nine years here.

Harvey's 1950 Petite Champagne landed 1964, bottled 1969.
Not so much early-landed, as late-bottled.

Hine 1953 Grande Champagne landed 1954, bottled 1971.
A true early-landed, late-bottled brandy.

Peter Dominic list:

Hine 1948 Grande Champagne landed 1949, bottled 1971.
Another true early-landed, late-bottled brandy.

Whereas other firms, who ought to know better, list some fine old brandies with vintage and bottling dates, but without any landing date, so that one does not know whether they have matured in a 'wet' English or a 'dry' Cognac bond. Which is how I once disappointed myself, leaping with delight on a great old country wine-merchant's list in which I spotted a famous firm's cognac with a forty-odd-year-old vintage date. I bought more than I could afford, only to find it too dark, coarse and woody for my taste, especially as I had been preparing my palate for the softness of early-landed, and high in alcohol into the baragain— save that it was no bargain. It was late-bottled, but not at all early-landed.

On the other hand, in 1968 I bought a half-hogshead of 1964 Delamain Grande Champagne, its vintage year still certifiable, which is now in bond in Bristol awaiting expert advice on when to bottle. If I do not live to see the day, some not too remote descendant may call down a blessing upon me for landing it early to have it bottled late.

9. The 'Napoleon' Legend

ONCE I had set up as a writer about wine, I began to be bombarded with letters from readers, and buttonholed at parties by acquaintances, who had bottles of 'Napoleon' brandy that they had been told were worth £1,000 apiece. Here, I would be told, or shown, was a cutting from a local newspaper about just such a bottle belonging to a neighbour—a neighbour who said that he knew for a fact that that was what it would sell for, but who would never part with it.

Was there not a cinema-owner in Leeds who had just such a bottle on display in the foyer, labelled with that very price, and solemnly and ceremoniously locked up in the safe at night?

Where, they besought me, could they dispose of their own bottles for a like amount? Some correspondents hinted tactfully

—some not so tactfully—at a commission; others, I fancy, expected me to jump at the chance myself, and must have been doubly disappointed, because not only did I keep my £1,000 in my pocket, but went out of my way, however gently, to disabuse them.

Some of the letters were pathetic—written by poorly-off and unworldly people who had, perhaps, been left by some old toss-pot of an uncle a bottle with an embossed 'N' and the date 1809 or 1811 and, half-ashamed of being remembered by the family scapegrace and even of having a bottle of strong waters in the house, saw in it, nevertheless, a trip to Majorca for the first time in their lives, or a piano in the parlour.

One reader, I recall, told me that the bottle was very dusty indeed, and assured me that she had been particularly careful not to clean it in any way, and thus detract from its value.

I wrote to each one as sympathetically as I could.

There was no such thing, I explained, as a true Napoleon brandy. If any did still exist, if it had been in wood since Napoleon's (the first Napoleon's) time it would now be undrinkable, because brandy deteriorated in cask after about seventy years. If in bottle, it would be only as good as *when* it was bottled, no better, because, unlike wine, brandy ceases to develop once it is in glass. If an 1809 brandy had been bottled, say, in 1829, it would still be a twenty-year-old brandy.

Eventually, I wrote an article that was published in the *Observer* of 8 April 1962:

THE NAPOLEON MYTH

'It is astonishing that the myth of "Napoleon brandy" still persists. Every serious writer about wine has inveighed against what Mr Warner Allen once referred to as "the vague Napoleon so light-heartedly attached to brandies of doubtful lineage", and again as "catch-penny frauds", adding that "even supposing that they were bottled during either the First or Second Empire, spirits do not improve in the glass, but go downhill slowly and surely".

'Yet only the other day there was a story in a popular paper about "a bottle of Napoleon brandy, vintage 1811", worth

Imp A Bellier . Bord .

LE FLÉAU

Depose

Dise - m'don c'qu'a fait queurver tielle vigne, de même !
Y disant qu'ol est ine insecte, in diable, in phylloc-scélérat, sais-j'y. counme il appelant thieu !... ol est teurjou
maufaisant !

7. A contemporary cartoon by Gautier of the peasantry's dismay at the
disaster of the phylloxera

8. A bottle of the so-called 'Napoleon Brandy' recently sold at Christie's. (*See* Chapter

£1,000, and kept in a safe every night; and a reader has written to me about his bottle of 1809.

'Mr Warner Allen could have added that not only do spirits deteriorate after years in bottle, but that they do not live for ever in wood, either: I have tasted a genuine 1870 in Cognac, straight from the cask, and very "woody" it was—it was kept as a sort of museum piece.

'The origin of the so-called 1809 and 1811 brandies, according to Maurice Healy's "Stay Me With Flagons", is this. There was a time when the firm of Bisquit Dubouché advertised "apparently unlimited quantities of their 1865, their 1834 and even their 1811. After 129 years" (this was written in 1940) "there could hardly be more than a tiny supply of an unrefreshed 1811, and I am sure that they do not wish their advertisements to be read as anything but an offer to supply a brandy blended to match the original 1811."

'The admirable firm of Bisquit Dubouché don't make such offers nowadays: their agents here tell me that it is generally recognised that after seventy years of topping-up to make good the loss by evaporation there is precious little left of an original old brandy, so that nothing earlier than something in the 1890s would survive in an old "refreshed" brandy. But some of those "1809" and "1811" brandies of a generation ago seem still to be about, inherited from forebears who are now fondly supposed to have inherited them from theirs. Not at all: they had bought for a guinea or thirty shillings or so a brandy that bore a date in the same way that a sherry can bear a *solera* date—the date, that is, not of a single vintage, but of the earliest element in the blend, however small. And it isn't worth £1,000, or keeping in a safe.'

Any hopes I had had that this might put paid to the myth were soon dissipated—any ideas I had had, too, that it was only my more credulous readers that had been taken in, and that the wine trade, at any rate, knew better. For my editor received a letter from a wine-merchant in Pinner (now deceased) that ran thus:

'Dear Sir.

'After reading the article headed "Napoleon Myth" by Mr

Cyril Ray in The Observer Week-end Review on the 8th instant, I, as owner of the now famous £1,000 bottle of Napoleon Cognac, would like to publicly explode this myth through the columns of your Newspaper, by saying that Mr Ray must be a professional writer on Wines and Spirits, for no other person would have the audacity to set himself up as an expert after reading a couple of chapters on Cognac one by Maurice Healey and one by H. B. Warner Allen, and then give an opinion on 1811 Cognac if he has only tasted one, and that of 1870.

'There is so much "balderdash" written these days on the subject of Wines and Spirits by professional writers that I think it would be refreshing if the public could now and again be able to read articles on Wines and Spirits by professional Wine and Spirits Merchants rather than professional writers.

'In February last year I was in Jarnac and was fortunate to taste at least ten cognacs ranging from 1805 to 1890 and found all but one, namely 1825, were still superb—and very drinkable.

'To explode the next myth, my own bottle of 1811 Cognac is not kept in a safe but has been displayed in the windows of several of my branches and is this very week on display in my shop window at Beaconsfield in Buckinghamshire.

Yours faithfully,'

To which I replied:

'Dear Sir,

'The editor of the Observer has passed on to me your letter about my article, "The Napoleon Myth".

'I didn't know that you, too, possessed a "now famous £1,000 bottle of Napoleon Cognac"—the one I referred to as being kept in a safe at night is being exhibited in his cinema foyer by a Leeds cinema-owner, and I have had letters from a number of readers who possess similar bottles.

'As for my "audacity" in giving an opinion on the "1811 Cognac" after reading Maurice Healy (not "Healey") and Herbert (not "H. B.") Warner Allen, let me quote some other authorities—"professional Wine and Spirits Merchants rather than professional writers", whom you rightly consider to carry more weight:

'A director of the firm that ships Bisquit Dubouché, whom I telephoned before I wrote the article in question: "No, of course, Bisquit Dubouché no longer market bottles purporting to contain 1809 or 1811 or 1865 brandy: it is now generally agreed in the trade that any brandy more than about 70 years old would have had to be "refreshed" so much by younger spirits that it could no longer claim the earlier date.

'M. André Simon (thirty years in the wine trade before he founded the Wine and Food Society)—in conversation over luncheon when I was planning the Observer article: "Napoleon brandy? Rubbish! There's no such thing."

'A director of the firm that ships Martell brandy, whom I telephoned today: "It would be most unlikely that it is a genuine 1811, and if it were it would be undrinkable."

'A director of the firm that ships Rémy Martin, whom I telephoned today: "No, of course you weren't writing 'balder-dash' in your article: you couldn't have a bottle full of 1811 brandy that would be drinkable. . . . The sooner this idea is quashed, the better."

'Do you want any more opinions from brandy-shippers? I could give you twice as many again, but let's go on to books other than those by Maurice Healy and Warner Allen:

' "Wines of France" (Cassell, 5th edition, 1961), by Alexis Lichine, both a wine-grower—in Burgundy and in the Médoc—and a wine-shipper, p. 255: "There is no real Napoleon Brandy on sale anywhere today, and even if there were, it would not be so good as an old Cognac bottled yesterday. The name is false and purposely misleading."

' "A Book of French Wines", by the late Morton Shand (revised edition, Cape, 1960), p. 313: " 'Napoleon' Cognac is a . . . deceptive description."

' "The French Vineyards", by Denis Morris (Eyre & Spottiswoode, 1958), p. 184: "The words 'Napoleon brandy' and an aged-looking bottle mean little or nothing . . . if in fact the brandy had been distilled in or before 1815 and had not been bottled within fifty or at the most sixty years it would have quickly deteriorated and all its alcohol would by now be merely a stain on the wall in Cognac."

*   *   *

'I have just spoken on the telephone to Mr Tom Taylor-Restell, head of the firm of W & T Restell, the only wine-auctioneers.[1] He says that whenever a story appears in the press about one of these alleged Napoleon brandies being worth £1,000 a bottle he gets letters from people all over the country, some direct and some forwarded by Christie's and Sotheby's, asking him to sell such bottles. He describes it as "a pain in the neck" to his firm, and it is, of course, an unkindness to lead people—some of them very hard-up—to believe that they possess such a treasure, when in fact Taylor-Restell has to tell them that such a bottle is worth about £8 to £10 and, he says, "is no more an 1811 than it's a No. 11 bus". On January 26 of this year he sold a *magnum* labelled "Grande Fine Champagne Impériale Napoléon 1811", and embossed with a crowned "N": it fetched £20.

'It is one thing to express polite disagreement with a writer on one's own subject, but there can seldom have been less justification for an attempt to damage the professional reputation of a serious journalist by writing to his editor that he wrote "balderdash", and using such phrases as "no other person would have the audacity to set up as an expert": I think you owe me an apology.

'If, on the other hand, you would like to send your "now famous £1,000 bottle of Napoleon Cognac" to a Restell sale, and it does in fact fetch £1,000, *I* shall be happy to apologise to *you*, and in print.

Yours faithfully,'

I did not have to apologize, but let us not suppose that my friend in Pinner was out for the count.

We next find him on Christmas Eve, 1965, being interviewed on the BBC's programme 'Today', because he now figured in the

---

[1] Absorbed by Christie's in 1966.

Guinness Book of Records (he is still in the latest edition) as having
sold four bottles of Napoleon brandy for £1,000 apiece, and as
now negotiating a fifth.

He had changed his tune, but only a little. Asked about the
bottles he had sold, he no longer claimed authenticity for them,
but still thwacked the unfortunate writers about wine: now, it
was they who had led the poor public astray:

'*Wine-Merchant*: Well I have been a wine merchant for many
years and I have been serving the public direct for 20 years.
And I came to the conclusion that there is so much nonsense
written by professional writers on the subject, and the public
being so gullible have believed it for so long, here was the
chance of seeing how gullible they really were.

'*Interviewer*: So in other words you're trading purely and
simply on the snobbery of wines and spirits.

'*Wine-Merchant*: Exactly.

'*Interviewer*: Well look, is this brandy ever going to be drunk
or do you think it's going to be just brought out, dusted off,
for the right occasion—some smart dinner party and stag
party—as the great wonderful status symbol?

'*Wine-Merchant*: I'm absolutely convinced that it is solely a
thing for snobbery. It will be brought out on the special
occasion, to be shown off, and then put back in the cobwebs
again.

'*Interviewer*: Well, have you ever drunk it yourself?

'*Wine-Merchant*: Not the specific bottles I've sold, no. But I
have tasted 40 brandies from 1805 to 1875, and of those I
would say 35 were superb and 5 were undrinkable.

'*Interviewer*: Well that one lying over there looks very dusty
and may very well be its age. But that may well be one of those
that are undrinkable; on the other hand, it may even only
contain water. How do you know it doesn't?

'*Wine-Merchant*: I don't. And aren't I lucky that there is such
snobbery that nobody else seems to be worrying about that?

'*Interviewer*: And people are prepared to spend a thousand
pounds for that snobbery.

'*Wine-Merchant*: Well it seems to be that way at the moment.

To date I've sold two bottles that were handled by solicitors for people, a third bottle was purchased and presented to the Madrid Drink Museum in my name, and the fourth bottle was sold to a millionaire. I think though they've fallen on hard times recently. I noticed that they're now trying to sell their yacht.

'*Interviewer*: But not the brandy.

'*Wine-Merchant*: No. Well at least they can get the brandy in the house.'

The fifth bottle was never sold. The wine-merchant died only a few days after his BBC interview, and in 1968 his widow (I now quote the current *Guinness Book of Records*) put the price up to £1,000 5s 4d, to cover an increase in the spirits duty and then—wisely, I think—withdrew it from offer.

* * *

Auction prices have gone up (and not only for cognac) since I wrote my *Observer* article in 1962. But the highest recorded even now is £130, paid at Christie's at the end of 1972—quite a lot of money for a bottle of brandy, but still a long way short of that £1,000 of seven years ago or more, and representing no greater rise over the saleroom prices of £8 or £10 that fine claret has shown over the same period. In any case, Michael Broadbent, head of Christie's wine department, told me that the present average is more usually around £50 ($124).

Since the autumn of 1966, Christie's have sold more than two hundred such bottles, labelled variously 'Maison de l'Empereur', ' "Napoléon" Grande Fine Champagne Réserve', 'Grande Réserve de l'Empereur' or, simply, 'N'.

With this amount of experience, Mr Broadbent has been able to evolve another theory about the origin of what he calls 'these Napoleonic nonsenses'—a theory that lifts some, at any rate, of the blame that has been put upon the Bisquit-Dubouché of half a century or so ago.

None of the couple of hundred bottles that have come Christie's way has borne a distiller's name—nor that of a vineyard or a grower, either. But one bottle was labelled as having been bottled in Cognac in 1903, and as all the other bottles were similar, he believes that they were specially put up in Cognac for a sizeable de luxe trade, probably with Paris as its chief market-place, around the turn of the century—for a couple of decades before about 1912.

I have not tasted any of these brandies, nor do I propose to do so. I would do many things to enlighten, or even merely to entertain, my readers, but bidding up to £130, or even £50, at Christie's for a bottle of brandy of doubtful origin is not one of them.

Fortunately, Mr Broadbent was able to persuade himself that he owed it to Christies's to buy in a couple of bottles for tasting. 'Surprisingly good, albeit on the heavy side—quite a common style in those days,' was his report.

What, though, explains the special magic that the name Napoleon—meaning always the first Napoleon—exerts in the world of cognac?

As Count Burignot de Varenne of Augier said, when we puzzled over the problem, it would be different if it were Napoleon III. For whereas his uncle's Continental Blockade had severely damaged—had it not been for smuggling and licensing might well have ruined—the cognac trade, by cutting it off from its best market, Britain, the nephew had ushered in its golden age with the commercial treaty that he negotiated with Cobden.

It seems possible that a good deal of use *was* made of Napoleon III's name when he was popular in France and, especially, in Cognac. And it seems, too, that as his cult faded, while that of his uncle always remained bright, the one Napoleon became gradually merged into the other—that many a cognac firm's reminiscences of the nephew, on label and in brochure, have somehow become romanticized into those of the uncle. . . . .

Brian Roberts, in his *Ladies in the Veld*, quotes a Durban liquor store's advertising Courvoisier as 'the only brandy supplied to the late Emperor Napoleon III' in a Natal newspaper of April 1880. Everyone was frenchifying his shop windows for the Empress's arrival to visit the scene of her son's death in action, but I cannot imagine that the keeper of a Durban liquor-store of the time would have dreamed up the connection between

Napoleon III and Courvoisier: the material must have come from the firm. The interesting point to my mind being that this is earlier than Courvoisier themselves tell me was the birth of 'The Brandy of Napoleon' as their advertising slogan, and the unmistakable figure—hand in coat, cocked hat on head—of the firm's trademark. No sad *revenant* this, from Sedan, but the victor of Austerlitz.

However that may be, Courvoisier managed to unearth, just in time for the pretty booklet they published to celebrate the bicentenary of Napoleon's birth in 1769, what, to be fair, is described as 'doubtless only a little anecdote, but at least it has the merit of being an Imperial one!' The merit, too, of justifying, if only *post hoc*, the bees and the laurelled 'N' on packaging and on labels; the imperial eagle on the carton that holds the representation boxes of Extra Vieille; the imperial artillerymen on the carton that holds a presentation bottle of three-star mounted on a gun-carriage; the Empire furniture in the vast commercial building in Jarnac, and its imperial carpeting.

The story goes that:

'As Emperor of the French, Napoleon often had sent to him supplies of Brandy from the Cognac Region and when he went on a campaign a few bottles were always included in his baggage. Already for the Emperor, as for every one at that time, Cognac Brandy was considered the best obtainable. In July 1815, after his abdication, Napoleon, for a short while, thought of leaving secretly for the United States. To this end the Minister of Police Fouché arranged for the victualling of two ships anchored in the little port of Fourras. The provisions put on board included Cognac supplied by Emmanuel Courvoisier.

'However, the Emperor quickly abandoned this escape project and decided to give himself up to the British. He set sail, therefore, for the Island of Aix in the Atlantic opposite Rochefort where the "Bellérophon" was awaiting him. Napoleon's belongings had consequently to be transferred to it but they were so voluminous that a second ship, the "Mirmidon", had to be affreighted. On both of these ships as far as

Plymouth, and on "H.M.S. Northumberland" as far as St Helena, the British Officers had numerous occasions to taste and enjoy this precious Cognac Brandy. In fact they appreciated it so much that, subsequently, they often spoke to their friends about the Emperor's Brandy and thus Courvoisier came to be known—in English—as "The Brandy of Napoleon".

'It followed that Courvoisier subsequently received in recognition an official warrant of appointment as Supplier to Napoleon III, and was thus often enjoyed at the Court of the Tuileries.'

The 'It followed . . . ' of that last paragraph is ambiguous, and I cannot myself recall having heard of 'The Brandy of Napoleon', in English, as dating from the abdication of 1815, but one way and another the name of the more glorious—if glorious is the proper word—of the two Napoleons has become inextricably linked with cognac. So much so that, as explained in the previous chapter, the law of the land has had to take cognizance of the fact—'Napoleon' must be every minute of five years old . . .

The delightfully absurd thing about it is that no firm that I know of that uses 'Napoleon' to denote one of its older and more expensive blends uses it for its oldest and most expensive.

Courvoisier themselves rank their Napoleon second to their Extra Vieille; so do Bisquit Dubouché—the two firms that have perhaps done most to promote the Napoleonic legend.

'It might just as well be Joan of Arc,' said one cynical shipper of my acquaintance, 'and in fifty years' time it'll probably be Charles de Gaulle.'

10. Cognac's Cousins and In-Laws

COGNAC and the sweet, prettily-coloured after-dinner liqueurs have a common ancestry. Before it was learned that brandy became palatable—and more than palatable—by being matured in wood, men wanted all the same to drink the raw, fiery spirit, for the warmth that it gave, or the alcoholic kick, or the courage, or all three.

Many, though, screwed up their faces or held their noses, as they tossed it down. How to make it more grateful to palate and to nose? The clues lay in what alchemists and monks had long been interested in, whether as magic or as medicine.

Strong waters could be made, or could be made to seem, health-restoring or passion-arousing, by the addition of herbs and sweetenings; colourings, scents and spices.

As Younger has put it,[1]

'Distillation had made them [liqueurs] possible and had changed the spiced and sweetened medieval drinks into the flavoured and sweetened spirits which are modern liqueurs.

[1] op. cit. pp. 386–7.

On the one side they trace their descent from Hippocras and on the other from the alchemists. . . . The most famous of them was the *rossolis* or *rossoly* which Fagon made for Louis XIV when his immense appetite began to impair his stomach, and which was generally drunk at dessert. This was made from the seeds of *anise*, and from fennel, dill, coriander and caraway, all of which were crushed and macerated for three weeks in a stoppered glass vessel. Spirits were then added together with water of camomile and sugar and the mixture, once it had been filtered, was ready for the royal patient. The liqueur was also held in esteem, though perhaps not for the same reason, by the king's subjects and in 1676 it was officially allowed to be sold on the streets of Paris. At the same time the street vendors were allowed to sell *populo* brandy and other liqueurs and essences. *Populo* was only a light, delicate *rossolis* and *rossolis* itself was for a time little more than a generic name for one class of liqueur based on brandy and sugar.'

Throughout the eighteenth century, brandy in general and cognac in particular became steadily more palatable, without benefit of spicing and sweetening, but a taste for the flavoured liqueurs, or *digestifs* (look what they had done for *le Roi Soleil*!) still remained in men's—or perhaps more particularly in women's—gastronomic memories. So they continued to be produced, more of them then than now based on brandy made from the grape, and in France much of the brandy used must have been from Cognac.

It would be remiss, then, not to mention in a book on cognac at least a representative few French liqueurs that are not only based on cognac, but that have links with the region itself.

First, and by right, the local liqueur.

I was tickled, as no doubt I was meant to be, by the advertisement published in the wine-trade press at the end of 1971 by Cusenier's London agent.

'What kind of company', they asked, 'stocks liqueurs nobody wants?' And went on:

'Sève Salençon is not one of the most popular liqueurs in the country.

'In fact, in the last three years, it has only been ordered once.

'A lady club-owner from the North sampled its delicate taste in France, fell in love with it, and when she came back promptly ordered a case . . .'

Going on, of course, to make the modest boast that Cusenier's agents had some, whoever else had not, and that they had done right by the lady from the North.

What amused me especially, though, was that when I then wrote to the firm for information about Sève, a name I had only just come across, as that of a cognac-based liqueur, in my researches for this book, it took them six weeks to send me a reply that began, 'After some investigation, we are able to give you the information required . . .'

What kind of a liqueur was it, I asked myself, that was not only unknown in this country, but that even the people who shipped it knew precious little about?

It is a curious anomaly that a liqueur based on cognac and, indeed, more than one brand of which is actually made in Cognac, should be as little-known as cognac is world-famous.

Gaston Courant, head of the small Cognac firm of Georges Courant that makes cognac-based liqueurs, told me that the peasants of the region used to make liqueurs that varied in style and in quality from farm to farm, based on their own cognac, and flavoured with whatever herbs and fruits came to hand.

In so far as these eventually came to be sold commerically, they were called *crème de cognac*, or even *crème à la fine champagne*, until the laws of appellation forbade the use of the words 'cognac' or 'fine champagne' in a title. The liqueur then became known as 'Sève', which means simply 'sap', and which is not a controlled appellation, though it is used, so far as I know, only for this particular type of product.

What is controlled by the laws of appellation is the use of the word 'cognac', not in the commercial brand-name—that is forbidden, anyway—but in the subsidiary description of the product on the label and in advertisements.

'*Au cognac*' signifies that a minimum of thirty per cent of the alcohol base must be cognac. (The rest may be neutral spirit.)

'*A base de cognac*' signifies a minimum of fifty per cent cognac.

'*Exclusivement au cognac*' signifies a hundred per cent cognac base.

The base of Monsieur Courant's Sève Patricia (or any name followed by '*cognac*' or '*de cognac*' such as Abricot Cognac or Sève de Cognac) is a hundred per cent cognac, the flavouring of Sève Patricia being a matter of herbs, fruit, sugar and, rather to my surprise, tea.

It is a sweet *digestif*, with no very distinctive flavour, but pleasant enough served cold after dinner in a small brandy glass, only about a quarter full. There are other brands to be found, none to my mind any better than Monsieur Courant's Sève Patricia—none, for that matter, any worse.

The same tiny firm makes no fewer than forty other liqueurs, the best of which to my mind is Sa'ala, a sweet coffee-cognac confection that should be served on crushed ice after dinner, like a crème de menthe, or, as at that very good Paris restaurant, Ledoyen, poured over ice-cream.

(My own experience is that any sweet liqueur based on cognac is none the worse for being 'cut', approximately half-and-half with its spirit base: one diminishes the cloying sweetness without, as a rule, losing anything of the flavour.)

Another liqueur based on cognac is Grand Marnier, as famous as Sève is little known. It is the most widely-sold of all French liqueurs (see '*Dossier d'Entreprise*', No. 27, October 1971) and to my mind, because of its character and true orange-cognac flavour, one of the three or four greatest of all after-dinner liquid sweetmeats.

It is made at Neauphle-le-Château, near Versailles, whither three times a week tankers carry 5,000 gallons of cognac a time. Grand Marnier, indeed, is so dependent on its supplies of cognac that there is a director of buying based on the region, with his headquarters five miles from Cognac, in the beautiful château of Bourg-Charente (which I wish the firm would restore and make more use of; there is a fine eleventh-century Romanesque church at Bourg-Charente, too, and an enterprising new restaurant).

This purchasing director, Maurice Braud, told me that the

firm sells a very little cognac, both three-star and VSOP—all blended from what he buys from grower-distillers and distillers —and a very little Cherry-Marnier, but eighty per cent of its production is Grand Marnier, *rouge* and *jaune*. These colours are not those of the two versions of the product, but of their packaging.

The *rouge* is what we know in this country, twenty per cent neutral alcohol and flavouring, eighty per cent cognac; the *jaune* is sold in France, Spain and the Scandinavian countries, cheaper because it contains no cognac, but only *eau de vie* from other parts of France.

In the brand of Grand Marnier that reaches our shores, the *rouge*, the flavouring is a spirit produced by steeping the peel of bitter oranges from Haiti with sugar in alcohol for two months; the cognac is approximately three years old and almost exclusively from the Grande and Petite Champagnes. Monsieur Braud says that he has tried Bois Ordinaires brandies in the past, and found that the quality of the liqueur suffered. Good Fins Bois brandies would be highly acceptable, but are hard to come by.

The region has taken Grand Marnier to its heart more closely than its own, more purely local, Sève: besides the ice-cream Grand Marnier and yoghurt Grand Marnier to be found pretty well everywhere in France, there is a *pâtisserie* in Jarnac that sells Grand Marnier cakes and pastries.

Another sweet liqueur I have a liking for is Bénédictine, but more particularly for B. and B., which stands for Bénédictine and brandy, a mixture the firm now makes up itself at Fécamp, in Normandy—the brandy, I am happy to say, being cognac.

B. and B. was first made for the American market. American bar-tenders and wine-waiters reported a demand for half-and-half Bénédictine and brandy; customers, in their turn, complained that often the poorest sort of 'domestic' brandy was used. The Bénédictine people decided to do the barman a good turn by providing the mixture ready-bottled, the customer a good turn by using not any sort of brandy but cognac, and themselves a good turn by making a profit on the whole drink instead of only a half of it.

Now, Bénédictine not only take half the output of the interesting little firm, Comandon of Jarnac, who supply Fécamp with a lightish, not too woody, three-year-old brandy, but have bought a majority holding, presumably for the sake of stocks, in the ancient family firms of Dor, Favraud and of Guy Gautier of Cognac (not to be confused with Gautier Frères of Aigre), founded in 1697, and conducted from a Dickensian office in one of the oldest of the cobbled streets that slope down to the river.

* * *

Pineau, and plums in brandy, are the delicacies that Barbet brings out for an honoured visitor to his house in Jarnac in Charles Morgan's *The Voyage*, set in the eighteen-eighties.

They might well be brought out by a Barbet of our own times, almost exactly a century later.

For centuries past, certainly since the sixteenth century, the peasants of the Charentes, like those of Champagne, have made an aperitif drink for themselves by 'muting' (checking the fermentation of) fresh grape juice by the addition of brandy. The ratafia of Champagne, the pineau of the Charentes, are sweet, strong, and tasty.

Pineau des Charentes has had an *appellation controlée* since 1935: it must be made of fresh juice from the grapes of the region, muted and fortified only by the brandy of the region.

There are sixty-odd substantial producers of pineau in the region, and many more smaller ones, most of them outside the central zones of the Champagnes, the Borderies and the Fins Bois, the brandies of which can be used more profitably than to make pineau. For similar reasons, none of the very biggest cognac houses makes pineau, though it is the biggest of those that do that make the best. Only they can afford the space and the capital to give their pineau a period of maturation in cask, which the law does not require, but which quality does.

It is not surprising, therefore, that the best pineaux I drank in Cognac (it is not a favourite drink of mine, but I think I know good from less good) were the Plessis of Camus and the Reynac of UNICOOP, both sizeable firms.

Cognac of the previous year is used, one of cognac to two of grape-juice, which may be red or white. The result is a bland drink, which does not smell so nice as it tastes; like the ratafia of Champagne, it is about as sweet and as strong as port and drunk in the same way by the Cognaçais—as a sweet, strong aperitif, served very cold.

At Camus, I was introduced by the son of the house, Philippe Camus, to a mixture of six of pineau to one of vodka, served very cold, the vodka cutting some of the sweetness, and I heard tell of, but did not try, a similar mixture that substituted kirsch for vodka. (Camus may well have thought of the vodka mixture because of their deal with the Soviet Union: they have the monopoly of the export of French wines and spirits to the Union and of the import of Soviet vodka into France. They are allowed to sell as much cognac there as they sell vodka at home.)

A finger of pineau in a tall champagne tulip, topped up with ice-cold fizz, is another tolerable tipple.

*   *   *

Gaston Courant preserves plums in pineau for a few private customers, but the custom of the country is to preserve fruit not in pineau but in cognac.

Fresh fruit in new brandy used to be the formula, and many households still stick to it, but a newcomer to the region has created a new Charentais speciality and, indeed, a new industry.

Lucien Breton, son of a Paris family firm specializing in *marrons glacés*, came to Barbezieux in 1963 to commercialize the traditional local custom of preserving fresh fruits in brandy by doing it the confectioner's way—by cooking the fruits, so that his are *fruits confits* in cognac.

Now, he has a model factory on the outskirts of the charming little town, employing two hundred girls all the year round, and as many as six or seven hundred more when the chestnuts come in from Italy and the clementines from Spain—after the vintage, fortunately, so that the extra labour is easy to get.

Except for these fruits, most that he uses are frozen—the raspberries, for instance, which are the favourites on the United Kingdom market: they are steam-cooked, and put with sugar syrup into jars of colourless one- or two-year-old cognac bought from Martell, so that Monsieur Breton's prettily-packed glass jars are labelled with the name of the fruit, followed by the phrase, *'un vrai fruit au cognac Martell'*. And Monsieur Breton makes something of a point of his being a *maître-confiseur*, and that his fruits are not just preserved in cognac—they are *confits*.

These delicious confections are expensive, but they are so rich that a little goes a long way—one whole chestnut or apricot, or a half clementine, in the appropriate amount of syrup is enough for most people at the end of a meal. And they are splendid with ice-cream.

In less than nine years, Monsieur Breton has reached an annual output of half a million litres of fruit, apart from the *marrons glacés* that he still produces, in Barbezieux as in Paris. He has also shown the way and set the pace for other firms, one of which preserves in Hennessy, as he does in Martell, and another of which, Ricard (no connection with the great aperitif house that now controls Bisquit-Dubouché), presents its *fruits confits* in a Grande Fine Champagne, no less.

Not only all this, but Monsieur Breton is also the moving spirit behind that admirable establishment, Prestige des Charentes, a pretty pavilion on the Angoulême-Barbezieux road, about twenty miles from Cognac, which no visitor should miss. Here you can taste three or four different pineaux and a dozen cognacs from various houses, at very modest prices; probably be given (it seems to be a matter of chance) a free sample of a Breton fruit; browse among examples of local arts and crafts; buy very good pâtés and other local delicacies in tins, and the superb local butter. Or simply, on a hot day, look in for a cold beer that was brewed the breadth of France away, and know that you will not be pestered to do more to support local industry, which makes it all the more civilized a shop-window for a very civilized region.

11. Golden in the Glass

J ust as cognac does not improve in bottle so, by the same token, it does not deteriorate. Unopened, it does not matter how long you keep it, or whether it is kept in a hot cupboard or in a cold cellar. Nor does it mind, as a fine wine would, being shaken up in the boot of a car, or the hands of a clumsy wine-waiter.

Is it worth keeping bottles of brandy in the cellar, when we are told that it does not improve in bottle? Apart from the fact that it does not deteriorate either, it is well to remember that nothing ever goes down in price. Cognac is expensive now, but it may well become more so, and a bottle put away today may save a few pence or a pound or so next year. And Henri Exshaw, head of his family firm which matures its cognacs in Bordeaux, once held forth to me on the subject, saying, 'Well, it doesn't actually *improve*, but it *does* settle down. Cognac is a blended product, and the longer the various elements are together the more completely they merge. Like an old married couple—neither may get any better-looking with age, but they do get used to each other. In a good marriage, they get more like each other in habits and even in looks—same thing with the various elements in a good blend.'

The one thing to remember in storing bottles of brandy for any length of time is that, unlike bottles of wine, the corks of which must be kept moist to remain healthy, they must be stood upright: spirits attack cork and rot it.

As for bottles that have been opened, this is another matter. Cognac does not change in an unopened bottle because it is not exposed to the air: once the cork has been drawn and the cognac poured there is more, and fresher, air between cork and liquid, and this will have an oxidizing effect.

Such effect on a three-star brandy would be negligible for many weeks, for the brandy is young—indeed, what little change there would be is likely to be for the better.

But it was François Chapeau, the *maître de chai* at Martell, who pointed out to me that he and his peers in other great firms had blended their VSOP and older brandies to be just in balance when bottled, and that even a modest further oxidization would throw that balance out. His advice—and no one's could be more worth having—is that once a bottle of VSOP or finer liqueur brandy had been opened, the unconsumed contents should be decanted into smaller bottles, with as little space left as possible, though without contact, between cognac and cork. Otherwise, a liqueur brandy left for more than a few days with a considerable air space (what the wine-shippers call 'ullage') begins to lose life and flavour, though its acidity increases.

Mind you, this is a Frenchman speaking, and a Cognaçais at that. The loss of life and flavour he refers to may be related in some way to the softness that Englishmen find agreeable, and the French find mawkish, in brandies matured in wood in England—'late-bottled' or 'early-landed' brandies (see pp. 108–110). Perhaps there is room here for experiment—myself, I can never keep a bottle of liqueur brandy open for long enough without finishing it to be able to decide whether, after a time, it begins to resemble an early-landed brandy or not . . .

Virtually all cognac-lovers, and certainly everyone in Cognac, talks of three-star brandy as suitable only for mixing as a long drink. Ask in a café in Cognac for any brandy by name and you are automatically served with a VSOP. If you want a three-star you must ask for it specially.

Of course, a VSOP is preferable as a liqueur, but one can be too high-and-mighty about the three-star of a reputable house. I have finished off many a meal in provincial England with such a one, neat with my coffee, and been genuinely grateful. It is not that three-star is an inferior cognac: it is simply that the older ones are even better.

All the same, if cognac *is* to be mixed, then three-star is the quality for mixing: the higher ranks must be treated with greater deference, when drunk as what the French call a *digestif* after dinner.

Let an English novelist be our first guide:

Franklin Blake, whom I suppose to be the hero (unless I am doing an injustice to Sergeant Cuff, English fiction's first detective) of Wilkie Collins's *The Moonstone*, asks the butler whether on the night of the theft he could possible have been drunk.

Betteredge replies that as he looked wretchedly ill, he was persuaded to take a little brandy-and-water, and Franklin Blake says,

 ' "I am not used to brandy-and-water. It is quite possible. . ."
 ' "Wait a bit, Mr Franklin. I knew you were not used, too. I poured you out half a wineglassful of our fifty-year-old Cognac; and (more shame for me!) I drowned that noble liquor in nigh on a tumblerful of cold water. A child couldn't have got drunk on it, let alone a grown man." '

Here, then, is a lesson to us—our first lesson. It is shame upon us to drown in cold water what Betteredge the butler rightly calls a noble liquor. A liqueur brandy is to be drunk neat.

Wilkie Collins published *The Moonstone* in 1868, though it was set in the eighteen-forties.

Our second lesson beginneth with a novel published in the nineteen-forties, though here, too, the significant scene is earlier still.

It was, according to the plot, some time between the wars that Charles Ryder, in Evelyn Waugh's *Brideshead Revisited*, took Lady

Julia Flyte's rich, hairy-heeled husband, Rex Mottram, to
Paillard's in Paris for dinner. Mottram lit his first cigarette
between the sole in a white wine sauce and the *caneton à la presse*—
which meant also on this occasion between the 1906 Montrachet
and the 1904 Clos de Bèze—and then:

'The cognac was not to Rex's taste. It was clear and pale
and it came to us in a bottle free from grime and napoleonic
cyphers. It was only a year or two older than Rex and lately
bottled. They gave it to us in very thin tulip-shaped glasses of
modest size.

' "Brandy's one of the things I do know a bit about," said
Rex. "This is a bad colour. What's more, I can't taste it in this
thimble."

'They brought him a balloon the size of his head. He made
them warm it over the spirit lamp. Then he rolled the splendid
spirit round, buried his face in the fumes, and pronounced it
the sort of stuff he put soda in at home.

'So, shamefacedly, they wheeled out of its hiding place the
vast and mouldy bottle they kept for people of Rex's sort.

' "That's the stuff," he said, tilting the treacly concoction till
it left dark rings round the sides of his glass. "They've always
got some tucked away, but they won't bring it out unless you
make a fuss. Have some."

' "I'm quite happy with this."

' "Well, it's a crime to drink it, if you don't really appreciate
it."

'He lit his cigar and sat back at peace with the world; I,
too, was at peace in another world than his. We both were
happy. He talked of Julia and I heard his voice, unintelligible
at a great distance, like a dog's barking miles away on a still
night.'

It will already, I hope, be clear to the reader what merit there
must have been in that cognac that was first offered—'clear and
pale . . . only a year or two older than Rex' (who was, I suppose,
in his thirties). It was especially meritorious of Paillard's to have
a cognac 'lately bottled'—late-bottled cognacs, as I have shown,
are only fairly frequent in England, and rare indeed in Paris

restaurants even of the noblest sort. (But Evelyn Waugh was right in referring to 'lately-bottled' and not to 'early-landed'. The terms are sometimes used indiscriminately, but a 'lately-bottled' cognac *could* be found in France, 'early-landed' only in Britain.)

So, too, was it praiseworthy to offer it in 'very thin tulip-shaped glasses of modest size'. Better men, and nicer men, than Rex Mottram have taken their brandies in balloons the size of their heads, but it is a mistake, none the less. Not that one advocates one of those piddling little so-called 'liqueur glasses' that have to be filled to the brim for one to enjoy even a modest mouthful, but one needs a glass big enough only to be filled one-third or one-quarter full when a decent measure of brandy (what an English pub would call a double, say) is poured in and, ideally, narrowing a little towards the top, so that the fragrance of the spirit is not only trapped, as it were, but directed and concentrated towards the nose. (These are the right glasses, too, for the dry fruit *eaux de vie*, such as calvados and kirsch, and for the jewel-bright sweet cordials, such as Chartreuse and cherry-brandy.)

At Lasserre, at least as good a real Paris restaurant as Paillard's is intended to be an imaginary one—to me, it is perhaps the greatest restaurant in Europe—they serve their superb cognacs in moderate-sized, slightly tapering glasses very like sherry *copitas*, if not perhaps quite so narrow at the top, and this is the type most favoured in Cognac itself, whether in the tasting-rooms or at table. (See drawing a. opposite.)

Virtually the only other shapes to be met with (though not so frequently) amongst the Cognaçais are what they call a tulip(b) and a very small *ballon*(c) of roughly the same capacity as either of the other two.

I have never seen one of those big goldfish-bowl balloons in the hand of anyone who distils or blends or ships serious cognac.

All glass from which one drinks fine wine or good cognac should be thin, but there are many who will say that this is especially important in a brandy glass because the liqueur must be gently warmed by the heat of the hand. This is the view most

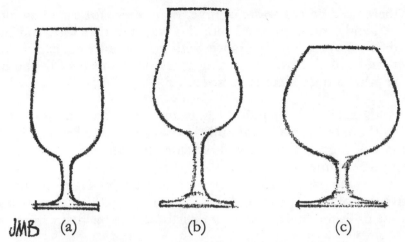

JMB   (a)   (b)   (c)

generally held by amateurs, and advocated by most of the great cognac houses themselves. Indeed, the small *ballon* is meant to be of a size that can just comfortably be completely cupped in the hand.

Thus, Charles Walter Berry, a dedicated wine-merchant and a great lover of fine wines and brandies, who lived in the age of fancy writing on the subject, laid it down in his *Viniana* (1929) that:

> 'Liqueur Brandy . . . should be served in suitable glasses, tulip-shaped and light in weight, not too large, and in no circumstances in those stupid oddities known as Liqueur Glasses. The stem should be slender, and when the priceless nectar has been served, the glass should be held in the right hand between the second and third fingers until such time as the Brandy has taken the warmth of the touch . . .'

At first reading, I took the old boy to mean that the bowl of the glass was to be held between two finger-tips, but one has only to try that operation with the second and third fingers to realize its impossibility. What he meant, of course, was that the stem of the glass was to be slipped between these fingers: in other words, the glass was to be cupped in the palm.

He went on:

> '—that is the ideal temperature. While it is being obtained,

there need be not waste of time, *au contraire*, for the glass can be gently turned in the hand, this way and that way, and by thus enjoying the fragrance with its stimulating effect the senses will give timely warning to all the members of the body of what a treat there is in store . . .'

And, similarly, Martell's handsome brochure advises, 'the glass should be warmed carefully in the palm of the hand and the aroma of a good Cognac will develop; it will even linger for a long time in the empty glass'.

But there are dissentients, none more forthright in their advocacy of the opposite opinion than the similarly distinguished house of Rémy-Martin, who in their brochure maintain stoutly:

'It is widely believed that it is correct to warm the brandy contained in a balloon glass in the hollow of the hand. There is even an element of snobbery attaching to the procedure. Professional tasters, while allowing everyone to drink his brandy as he pleases, disapprove strongly of this method. It has, indeed, one serious disadvantage: the more superior its quality, the more strongly does the warmed brandy give off a powerful aroma which induces a real anaesthesia of the faculties of taste and smell. The balloon glass, with its funnel-like effect, accentuates still more this regrettable effect. Warming a balloon glass in the hollow of the hand is of use only to bring out the quality of second-rate brandies, from which an aroma may thus be forced.

'A good brandy like Rémy Martin's Fine Champagne VSOP contains subtle perfumes which can be inhaled and appreciated even when it is iced. And so we suggest to connoisseurs this test to genuine quality which consists of drinking brandy only in glasses the form of which has been chosen by professional tasters. These glasses are almost straight, and tall enough to be used only a third full, leaving the top free to collect the most subtle and gratifying vapours. The true-brandy lover, if he so wishes, may make a test by adding an ice cube in the glass, which will emphasize still more the incomparable fine quality of Rémy Martin Cognac.'

When experts differ so widely as this, we amateurs may surely regard ourselves as at liberty to go each our own idiosyncratic way. Myself, I am more—much more—for the hand-warming than for the icing, which to my mind numbs fragrance and flavour, but I agree whole-heartedly with Evelyn Waugh's implicit condemnation of the spirit-lamp. If one's taste is like mine, then the warmth of the hand is quite adequate for cognac, as it is for claret: warmed on a spirit-lamp the glass becomes too hot, and releases the fine fragrance of its contents too violently. And to burn methylated spirits in the presence of a fine brandy is, in any case, an act of consummate lunacy.

* * *

For further refinements—though few of us, I fear, are so dedicated as this—I commend those interested to the practice in the tasting-room at Hine (and, I am sure, of most other firms of the same meticulous sort, but it was at Hine that I recorded the details in my note-book).

The fine, thin Baccarat glasses are washed only in distilled water and are then hung upside down to drain themselves dry—never wiped, lest even the finest linen cloths impart a lingering flavour or aroma to the glass. The girls who sweep the floor are forbidden to touch the glasses (or the tasting bench, come to that: only a member of the Hine family may wash a glass, or clear the table), which are rinsed, inside and outside, in the cognac one is to taste before one tastes it.

We have been discussing liqueur cognac, of course—the VSOPs and better, as explained in chapter 8.

The same sort of glass is used for the *trou charentais*, or *coup de milieu*, the glass of cognac served as a digestive and to give a breathing-space between the main courses of important public dinners in the region and at bucolic banquets, in the way that calvados is served as a *trou normand*, or that sedater folk serve a sorbet. But the custom is dying out: I have come across it only once myself. Even at French banquets, the courses are not so many or so heavy as they used to be.

* * *

There is no need to be so pernickety about what glass to use for cognac as a long drink, or as an aperitif, or, indeed, as medicine—the usual three-star, or similar quality and age, that is. Writing in his middle years of how, when he was eighteen, he had broken his bones and ruptured a kidney by jumping from a bridge on his aunt's estate and falling twenty-nine feet to the hard ground, the late Winston Churchill recalled[1] that Lady Randolph 'hurried down with energetic aid and inopportune brandy', but not the suitability or otherwise of the brandy glass.

(Unlike Bertrand Russell, who remembered all his long life how, as a boy of seventeen, in 1889, he chanced to be the only male member of the family at home when the eighty-year-old Mr Gladstone came to dine and stay the night. After the ladies had left the dinner table the boy waited—himself grandson of a prime minister—nervous but agog, for the pearls of wisdom that would surely fall from the aged statesman's lips. There was a silence, and then Mr Gladstone spoke:

'This is very good port they have given me, but why have they given it me in a claret glass?')

*   *   *

A tumbler, or what the Americans call a highball glass, is good enough for brandy and soda, and on the bridge of a destroyer in what was then Captain Mountbatten's Fifth Destroyer Flotilla of Js and Ks, under fire for the first time in what had hitherto been a sheltered life, I have drunk brandy-and-ginger ale from a chipped enamel mug and felt a little less cowardly in consequence.

The taste I then acquired has stayed with me sufficiently for it still to be my chosen tipple at theatre bars when I can fight my way to one at an interval. In other circumstances I now find the mixture too sweet, but it is no doubt the sugar that keeps one going from too early a dinner to too late a supper—sometimes even giving one the strength to battle one's way into that other kind of stall in a London theatre's invariably inadequate urinal.

The first time I visited Cognac, many years ago, I was surprised and amused to find my hosts, distinguished distillers and blenders of brandy, taking Scotch-and-soda before dinner while their

[1] Churchill, *My Early Life*, London, 1930.

English guests politely took the cognac of the house with water—*fine à l'eau*.

That was *le snobisme* of the time—Scotch is selling more widely now in France and, in consequence, has lost its *chic*.

Now, it is cognac or champagne as an aperitif (pineau, or pineau with vodka, say, is less likely)—the cognac usually with soda or with a bottled table-water. But at the hospitable house of a Hennessy director during my latest visit I was offered a mixture new to me—*cognac-orange*, which consists of two-thirds fresh orange juice and one-third cognac, served on the rocks as an aperitif, a sort of supercharged Buck's Fizz, save that it reverses the proportions (Buck's Fizz is two of champagne to one of orange) and is a good deal more potent. But deliciously refreshing and bracing after a long hot day.

I have heard tell of Americans who take their cognac with tonic, a mixture I have not tried, and do not propose to. There may well be those who take it with coca-cola, and I shall not try that, either.

As a long drink, I like brandy with soda, or with any sparkling table water, such as Perrier or Apollinaris (with the ice that I eschew with a liqueur brandy), and the French like their *fine à l'eau*, or brandy and tap-water, which I find a flat and mawkish drink. All the same, cognac served this way, with still or with sparkling water—or, indeed, with the orange-juice I have mentioned—makes a good aperitif because, being made from the grape, it is not going to quarrel with one's dinner-wine as whisky or gin or vodka can. Not that I am puritanical about mixing grape and grain, but like goes with like, and brandy seems to me to be more especially in keeping with wine, whether before or after, than other spirits.

'*Fine*' in a restaurant or a café, when one asks for a *fine maison*, *une fine*, or a *fine à l'eau*, does not mean what it is obliged to mean on a label: it is any house brandy. On the other hand, there are many a French cook and many a French housewife with recipes that require cognac in the sauce or the marinade or for a final flaming, and all such are worth serious attention.

It was one of the most distinguished of London restaurateurs who once told me, in a burst of confidence (which is why I do not give his name, or that of his restaurant), that what made even his luxurious *caravanserai* inferior to restaurants of similar rank in Paris was—to give an example, he said—that in his kitchen they used 'cooking' butter and 'cooking' brandy, because of the way his books were scrutinized by accountants and shareholders and the like, whereas in the kitchens of his opposite numbers in Paris, where even accountants and shareholders care as much about quality as about profit, they used the same brandy and the same butter for cooking that they served at table.

I did not take him to mean that it was liqueur brandy that went into the sauces in Paris, but that it *was* cognac, and not 'grape brandy'.

Does it make all that difference in the taste of a sauce? Perhaps not, but it makes an enormous difference to the moral of the chef and his *brigade*, and to their pride in their job.

This is not the place for a long list of recipes, whether for memorable dishes or for mixed drinks, but it would be remiss of me not to quote Eliza Acton's 1845 comment (remiss of me, because my wife edited Eliza Acton for readers of our own time) that her 'Very Superior Whipped Syllabubs' are 'considered less wholesome without a portion of brandy', and her recipe for a sort of forerunner of Irish coffee, but without the cream: 'Burnt Coffee, or Coffee à la Militaire (in France vulgarly called Gloria): Make some coffee as strong and as clear as possible, sweeten it in the cup with white sugar almost to syrup, then pour the brandy on the top gently over a spoon, set fire to it with a lighted paper, and when the spirit is in part consumed, blow out the flame, and drink the *gloria* quite hot.'[2]

Nor can I forebear to mention here that it is the addition of brandy to a champagne cocktail (which in itself consists only of champagne poured over a lump of sugar on to which have been shaken three drops of Angostura, with a twist of lemon or orange peel added) that transforms it into a Maharajah's Burra Peg, which is worth knowing about for when maharajahs come to dinner.

For lesser mortals, it would be nice to revive one of the classic

[2] Elizabeth Ray, *The Best of Eliza Acton,* selected and edited, London, 1968.

cocktails of the cocktail age—that period of cloche hats, Carpentier and the Co-optimists, Lenglen and the League of Nations, and of flat-bosomed flappers, between charlestons, gossiping over clover clubs or white ladies about the man that danced with the girl that danced with the Prince of Wales. All that is left to us is the dry martini, but the sidecar used to be regarded as the one mixed drink to take before a dinner at which fine wine was to be served, for it was brandy-based, with nothing more added than half as much fresh lemon-juice as brandy, and the same of any triple sec white curaçao, such as Cointreau, served ice-cold. Delicious!

Those who have wintered in Scandinavia must inevitably have come across Swedish glögg, for which I have seen many elaborate recipes. The simplest heats a quart of brandy into which have been put half a cup of sugar, a dozen cloves and a stick of cinnamon. When almost boiling (hot drinks must never boil) a pint of sherry is stirred into the mixture, which is then served in warmed mugs in each of which are a couple of raisins and of blanched, unsalted almonds. Port, madeira or claret can take the place of sherry, but nothing can replace the brandy.

Proportions may be altered, too, but it is as well to bear in mind the warning pronounced in 1862 by Jerry Thomas, the great New York bar-tender of a century ago, in writing about a similar concoction in his classic *How to Mix Drinks, or the Bon-Vivant's Companion*:

'This preparation is a very agreeable refreshment on a cold night, but should be used in moderation; the strength of the punch is so artfully concealed . . . that many persons, particularly of the softer sex, have been tempted to partake so plentifully of it as to render them somewhat unfit for waltzing or quadrilling after supper.'

The Viennese *Lebensretter*, or life-saver, is nothing more (or less) than a bottle of port to half a bottle of brandy, sugared to taste, and served hot.

The good book in which I first came across this noble brew, (I think it was an American 'Old Vienna Cookbook', so-called,) said that it was efficacious as a remedy for fainting spells, and

I can well believe it. The Wine Society calls it negus, and makes even more potent medicine of it, by recommending as much brandy as port, besides adding a splash of lemon-juice and a dash of spice.

But then, there is no end to the medicinal uses of the good creature.

My old, late, and much-lamented friend, Vyvyan Holland, who survived the savageries he suffered as a child, and wrote about so movingly in his *Son of Oscar Wilde*, to become a much-loved lover of life, used to tell of a great-uncle who kept a few fine bottles of rare old cognac for rare old friends. One day his house took fire and one fireman, in particular, behaved with great gallantry. The old gentleman could think of no more handsome gesture than to offer him a glass of this oldest and most noble brandy. The fireman, drenched by the hoses, sat down, took off his boots and socks and said, 'Thank you kindly, sir: a very happy thought. I'm a teetotaller myself, sir, but I've always found that there's nothing like brandy to stop you getting a cold', and poured the precious fluid over his feet.

12. Yesterday—And Tomorrow

W HEN George, Prince of Wales, first set eyes upon his bride-to-be, Caroline, in April 1794, he greeted her politely enough, but then turned immediately to Lord Malmesbury, who had escorted her from Brunswick, with, 'Harris, I am not well; pray get me a glass of brandy.'

We can be sure that the brandy was French, and pretty nearly as sure that it was cognac. For the trade between the Charentes and England had been in full swing ever since the Treaty of Utrecht reopened the ports to the brandies that had been maturing in oak during the War of the Spanish Succession.

It was still brisk, for all that we were at war again with France. Even as the Prince was calling for his brandy, and as his bride was murmuring to the same over-burdened Malmesbury, '*Je le trouve très gros*', the Prince's younger brother, our rare old Duke of York (he was every minute of thirty), was marching his ten thousand men up whatever hill the Low Countries afforded, and then down again lest worse befall them at the hands of the disconcertingly unconventional armies of the young French Republic.

Throughout the Revolutionary and Napoleonic wars, however, although the home market for cognac was disturbed, taxation heavy, and the export trade handicapped, especially after Napoleon's establishment of the Continental Blockade, the trade with Britain continued.

Nathaniel Johnston, of an Anglo-Irish family long settled in Bordeaux, and prosperous in the wine trade with Britain, wrote on 22 July 1801 that 'notwithstanding the War, business has been carried on with France for England via Guernsey and Ireland by neutral vessels which are admitted to Entry there coming direct'.[1] As I have written elsewhere, 'Wines and other commodities were carried in neutral ships—Danish, Dutch or American, as the various alliances broke and re-formed, and even French ships wearing American colours, carrying licences issued at a high price by the British Government, permitting the import through the Channel Islands of French wine and brandy; gloves, lace, prunes; and the juniper berries so necessary for the flavouring of London and Plymouth gin. It was with some justice that Napoleon called England a nation of shopkeepers, though the French, too, were very ready to make a profit out of trading with the enemy.'[2]

And what was not carried under licence was carried without: this was a high old time for smugglers.

One way and another, the cognac trade survived, and not only survived but prospered. And the end of the war meant better times still, especially after officers from the army of occupation returned from Paris, diplomatists from Vienna, with the taste of cognac still on their lips.

Some called it brandy, generally, some cognac, specifically, and had done for long enough. As long as forty years before the Prince of Wales's ill-starred confrontation with Caroline of Brunswick, and his call for brandy, simply, Commodore Hawser Trunnion was run away with by his horse on the way to *his*

[1] Quoted from Nathaniel Johnston's letter books, then in the possession of Messrs Davis and Hammond, in H. Warner Allen, *A History of Wine*, London, 1961.

[2] Ray, *Fide et Fortitudine: Langoa-Leoville Barton, 1821–1971* (printed privately for Mr Ronald Barton, 1971).

wedding, and had his marital capabilities restored by the admini-
stration of 'neat Cogniac' from a friendly flask.[3]

In each case the cognac is a restorative, as it still was almost
a century after Commodore Trunnion's time, when Jorrocks,
shivering before a jump, exclaimed, 'Fancy a great sixteen 'and
'oss lyin' on one like a blanket, or sittin' with his monstrous
hemisphere on one's chest; sendin' one's werry soul out o' one's
nostrils. Dreadful thought! Vere's the brandy?'[4]

In real life, there was 'old Bob Weild'—Captain Robert Weild
of the 69th Foot—who was so badly wounded in the Crimea that
nothing would have saved his life, he said, but the pint of
brandy that the regimental surgeon at once poured down his
throat. 'Thereafter', General Butler recalled, 'he lived by the rule
that if brandy could save a life it could also preserve it.'[5]

It is doubtful, though, whether old Bob Weild ever drank it
as an after-dinner liqueur. It is true that there are references in
the literature of the period to cognac as a *digestif*—Guy Living-
stone, the swaggering Life-Guardsman in G. A. Lawrence's
novel, published in the year of the Mutiny, takes 'one glass of
cognac, neat, as a *chasse*'—but throughout the eighteenth century
and most of the nineteenth it was much more likely to be port,
claret or madeira that the gentlemen lingered over at the end of
dinner.

Usually, until the turn of the century, cognac was taken as a
medicine or as a cordial—more as an *aperitif* than as a *digestif*—
or else as an ingredient for punches, neguses and toddies, hot or
cold, to spend the evening over after leaving the port in the
dining-room, and then to go to bed on. During the day, it was
taken as a long drink with soda—the celebrated 'B and S' of
Victorian literature and life.

Even so, there was always something of a class distinction
between cognac and the other spirits. True, John Jorrocks was
hardly what his fellow fox-hunting men would have called a
gentleman (neither were most of his fellow fox-hunting men,
come to that) but he was a rich and great city grocer, and could

[3] Smollett's *Peregrine Pickle*, 1751.
[4] R.S. Surtees, *Handley Cross*, 1843.
[5] W. F. Butler, *An Autobiography*, London, 1911.

well afford the brandy on which he and his huntsman so fuddled themselves that Pigg, sent to look out of the window to see what sort of night it is, makes the classic discovery that it is hellish dark and smells of cheese. But when Pigg gets pickled enough in the farmer's kitchen first of all to sing 'Weel may the keel row' and then to go to bed with his boots on, it is on Hollands and hot water.

Similarly, in another of what Rudyard Kipling called 'the natural-history books by Mr Surtees'—nobody is a better guide to the food, drink, clothes and general goings-on of the period— we find that after Facey Romford had entertained Soapey Sponge to a bachelor dinner *à deux*, it was 'well, now, what shall we have to drink? Shall it be gin, rum, or Hollands—Hollands, rum, or gin?' Whereas, staying with Sir Harry Scattercash at Nonsuch, Soapey finds himself ending the day with 'billiards, brandy and 'baccy'.

It was a golden age for the cognac trade and went on being so: 'the amount of B and Ss consumed in the 'seventies and early 'eighties was quite prodigious', Ralph Nevill recalled when he wrote his *Mayfair and Montmartre* in the nineteen-twenties.

Sales in the United Kingdom of French brandy, already booming, had boomed even louder after 1860, when Gladstone's budget, result of the commercial treaty that Cobden had negotiated with Napoleon III, brought down the duties on French wine and spirits to a 'most-favoured nation' level.

Cobden is still gratefully remembered in Cognac. What was once the Place Martell is now the Place Charles de Gaulle, but Rue Cobden still runs off the Avenue Victor Hugo—appropriately, just opposite the Chamber of Commerce, so that the local businessmen can look out at the street-sign, and call down blessings. The growers grumbled at first—Alfred de Vigny, trying to sell his Fins Bois, was among the grumblers—because the shippers were doing so well that they could afford to haggle over their prices, but the trade soon benefited as a whole.

For who in Britain would buy any other brandy but cognac, when cognac paid no more duty than any other? Such a boom resulted from the commercial treaty that three-quarters of the cognac houses existing today, I am told, were founded during the Second Empire, and the trade was comfortably cushioned against the decline in the translantic trade caused by the American Civil War of 1861–5.

So timely were the Cobden treaty and the Gladstone budget in their unwitting anticipation of the effects of the Civil War, that

AMERICA CONQUERED BY COGNAC

She took her revenge

the Cognaçais might well have supposed that they were the darlings of the gods—that nothing could go wrong for them. But America was still to exert a malign influence. In June 1863 Professor Westwood of Oxford was sent by a friend with a greenhouse in Hammersmith a vine-leaf from the United States that had puzzled him: 'it was covered with minute gall-like excrescences, each containing eggs and aphids'. In 1865 an 'unknown disease' struck vineyards in France. The aphids were plant-lice—the vine phylloxera, natives of North America. Revenge indeed, as Bertall has it in the drawing reproduced on the previous page, for cognac's having conquered that subcontinent.

George Ordish, author of the only book in English on the blight that cost France more than the war of 1870,[6] explained the phylloxera in a magazine article in the centenary year of its appearance in Hammersmith:[7]

'. . . there are a number of different species of vine in the world. The European species, *Vitis vinifera*, is the only one that gives good wine. Some of the American species (they are numerous) produce grapes in abundance, for instance the Northern Fox vine, *Vitis labrusca*, but all make very poor wine, with a strong "foxy" taste. The Phylloxera is an American insect, which lives mostly on the leaves of the American vines and does no great harm to them. It is able to inject some substance into the sap of the leaf that induces a gall to form and thus shelter the insect. The facts suggest a very ancient association between the American vines and the Phylloxera: they had evolved a form of peaceful co-existence. The insect lived mainly on the leaves, and not much on the roots, because certain vines had been selected out, by the forces of nature, with roots on which the Phylloxera could not flourish. The case was different with the European vines. *Vitis vinifera* had not evolved alongside the Phylloxera aphid, its roots had no built-in resistance. The Phylloxera attacked both leaves

[6] Ordish, *The Great Wine Blight*, London, 1972.
[7] *Land*, magazine of the Shell Chemical Co., Spring 1963.

and roots, though it liked the roots best; it formed the usual more or less harmless galls on the leaves but had disastrous effects on the roots. The substance it injected was very active: it produced distortions which soon killed the roots and the plant died.'

A PHYLLOXERA FAMILY, MAGNIFIED

The French first found the phylloxera at its deadly work in 1865, in Provence, and it was slow in working its way north. Although detected earlier it did not seriously affect the Charentes until after the warm summer of 1875 (in Champagne it was as late as 1890) by which time there was a fair amount of experience to draw upon: as Mr Ordish put it in a letter to me, 'The Cognac was very progressive vis-à-vis the phylloxera. Instead of screaming how hopeless, stingy and inefficient the Phylloxera Commission was, they set up their own research organization under a first-class scientist, Maxime Cornu, who got to the bottom of the complex life histories and the beast's different behaviour on French and American vines.

'I do not think the phylloxera did the Cognac much harm, that is to say the big houses and the *entrepreneurs* who, after all, are the only people who count! Due to their research station they overcame the pest quickly and in the meantime liquidated their vast stocks at high prices. This is only a feeling; I've not looked into it, but look at the houses standing in Cognac to this day and compare, say, pre- and post-1885 buildings. The labourers and small farmers starved and emigrated.'

True enough, if one allows for the irony behind the exclamation mark that follows 'people who count'. The pattern of the trade changed: many of the small men sold out, or moved out; big firms became bigger; the abuses of the time, as we have seen in chapter 5, led at length to the official delimitation of the cognac region and to legal protection for its name. Meanwhile, it took twenty years to re-plant those Charentes vineyards that *were* replanted (by no means all of them were) with vines grafted on to phylloxera-resistant American root-stock.

PROFILE OF A COGNAC MILLIONAIRE
How rich they were before disaster struck!

The changes I have outlined were not the only ones, nor were the changes that the blight brought about confined to France.

Winston Churchill wrote, in the tale of his adventures with the Malakand Field Force, that it was in September 1898, while waiting to go into action on the North-west Frontier, that he overcame his 're-pugnance to the taste of whisky', adding that 'to this day' (he was writing in 1930) 'I have never shrunk when occasion warranted it from the main basic standing refreshment of the white officer in the East'.

The point of the story, though, is that, as Winston Churchill pointed out, 'of course all this whisky business was quite a new departure in fashionable England. My father for instance could never have drunk whisky except when shooting on a moor or in some very dull chilly place. He lived in the age of the "brandy and soda".'

The change in fashion and in taste was not, as such changes often are, a matter of chance and of whim. It so happened that the distillers of Scotland had begun to blend into their aromatic single-malt whiskies, distilled, like cognac, in old-fashioned pot stills—whiskies suitable for grouse-moors, but too heavy for drawing-rooms—the lighter, drier, more nearly neutral, patent-still grain whiskies, just at the time that the effects of the phylloxera's invasion of the Charentes were beginning to take effect.

(The louse was first identified in the region in 1872 or 1873, but it was some years before it got a firm grip on the majority of the cognac vineyards, and some years, too, before pre-phylloxera stocks in Cognac and in the cellars of London wine-merchants began to run low. It must have been ten years or so before the brandy-and-soda habit was endangered.)

At first, patent-still grain whisky was looked at askance, and so, too, were blends of patent-still grain and pot-still malt.

The Distillers Company Limited, formed in 1877 by a combination of six Lowland grain patent-still distillers, battled against those who denied, in pamphlets and in Parliament, that grain whisky was entitled to be called whisky at all; against the book, *Truths about Whisky*, sponsored by Jamesons and Powers, still honoured names in Dublin, 'to check the practices of the fraudulent traders by whom silent spirit, variously disguised and flavoured, is sold under the name of Whisky'.[8]

The war rumbled on until the famous 'What is whisky?' case of 1905, but in effect it was won and lost in 1891, when a Select Committee reported that 'it is stated that public taste requires whiskey of less marked characteristics than formerly, and to gratify this desire, various blends are made, either by the mixture of pot-still products, or by the addition of silent spirit from the patent-stills. . . .' The committee concluded that the addition of patent-still spirit could be viewed not as an adulteration but as a

---

[8] 'Silent spirit' is neutral spirit—tasteless alcohol.

dilution and a legal act within the regulations as to the limits of strength of spirits.[9]

The heads of the 'big five' blended-whisky firms, men who began as their own commercial travellers, were well on the way to their peerages and their racing-stables.

Meanwhile, cognac itself was under a cloud, for by now, because of shortages caused by the phylloxera, this too was being adulterated, perhaps more in the cellars of London than in the *chais* of Cognac. It would be all the easier at this time because most cognac was shipped in cask, to be bottled and labelled by the importer, and usually under his name.

Denis-Mounié's books record a shipment on 22 March 1847 of a hundred cases of Old Pale Cognac Brandy to Messrs Sevill of London, and this may well be the first shipment of cognac to London in bottle. It became more frequent in the 1850s, when Cognac's first glass factory was established by a Monsieur Joseph, but by no means general until the 1890s—after, and perhaps because of, the scandals of adulteration in the period of dearth during the phylloxera plague.

In the pretty park of the Hôtel de Ville in Cognac is a waxed-moustached, four-in-hand cravatted bust, set up

A

CLAUDE BOUCHER

MAITRE DE VERRERIE

1842–1913

INVENTEUR DE LA MACHINE

A TRAVAILLER ET A SOUFFLER

LE VERRE

Claude Boucher's glassworks, founded in 1878, still stands, just outside the town, on the Saintes road; it belongs now to the vast Saint-Gobain firm, one of whose four factories, at Pont-à-Mousson, on the other side of Cognac, turns out more than a million bottles a day. There is a painting of the interior of Boucher's glassworks, as it was in 1910, in the Cognac museum,

[9] Nowadays we spell Irish whiskey with an 'e', Scotch whisky without. In these various quotations I have spelled the word as in the originals, and here what is the present custom has been reversed.

and the prototype of the bottle-making machine that he invented and put into service in 1898. The dates are significant.

*   *   *

The phylloxera; the doubtful brandies that found their way on to the British market; the new blended Scotch whiskies and their bustling salesmen—it might have spelled the end of brandy, and particularly of cognac, the finest of all brandies, but it did not.

True, the new sort of Scotch whisky not only retained the position it had won, but vastly extended it—always, though, as the basis of a long or a mixed drink: Scotch and water; Scotch and soda; Scotch, eventually, on the rocks.

But cognac made a magnificent come-back in a new and noble role as the lordliest of after-dinner drinks, challenging vintage port itself, as whisky had challenged brandy.

Partly, perhaps, because the emphasis was now, more than ever, on quality. Not all the vineyards of the Charentes were replanted. Particularly to the west, beyond Saintes, and to the east, beyond Angoulême, and in the Bons Bois zone generally— wherever the wines did not command prices as high as those of the two Champagnes and the Borderies, land that had been given over to grazing while diseased vines were uprooted tended to be left as such. The high quality and great repute of Charentais butter dates from this post-phylloxera period.

Rather less than 200,000 acres are now under vines in the Charentes—some twelve and a half per cent of the cultivated area of the region. In 1877, before the phylloxera had really got a hold, the French taxation authorities (working, in any case, probably on the previous year's returns) reported nearly 700,000 acres—more like thirty per cent.

Hence some of the trade's present problems.

Cognac is big business: in the 1971 edition of the list of France's five hundred biggest exporters published annually by the business weekly *Entreprise*, Martell lies ninety-second with 166 million francs worth of exports, Hennessy ninety-seventh with 163, Courvoisier one hundred and seventeenth with 131 million.

One way and another, by mergers, or majority holdings and the like, Moët and Chandon (who have many other interests, too) are now allied with Hennessy; Hiram Walker have moved in on Courvoisier; Ricard, the aperitif people, on Bisquit-Dubouché; and Cointreau on Rémy-Martin. Martini have gobbled up the less well-known firm of Gaston Legrange; Seagram have swallowed the time-honoured house of Augier, largely perhaps for the publicity value of its establishment date; and—ironic echo of the struggle of the eighteen-eighties—Distillers Company Limited now own the fine old cognac firm of Hine, long distinguished for its liqueur brandies. Only Martell, of the biggest houses, remains wholly independent.

Big business, yes: but, as Michel Martell pointed out to me, cognac is not an industrial product in the sense that whisky is. The whisky distillers can go anywhere in the world to buy the cheapest grain, of whatever kind they can find, and as much of it as they want. But cognac's raw material is limited—only grapes; only grapes of a certain kind; and only from a district severely delimited by law.

The sale of cognac in its home market went up from just under 10 million bottles in 1960 to 24·5 millions in 1971—a rise of nearly 150 per cent in twelve years, 'despite', says the official report, with understandable smugness, 'the recent vogue for, and the heightened competition from, various other spirits, especially from abroad'.

We in Britain, putting away no fewer than 16 million bottles in 1970–71, remained Cognac's best overseas customers, but the Americans and the West Germans, with 14 millions apiece and over, are now close on our heels. I can think of fellow-countrymen who will regard this as a challenge.

With this ever-increasing demand, the shippers press and press again for more planting to be permitted. For although only twelve and a half per cent of the cultivated area to the area entitled to the *appellation controlée* is under vines, this does not mean that the vines can be planted at will anywhere in the remaining eighty-seven and a half. Planting is rigorously controlled, inspected, and requires permission.

Every shipper I spoke to in the area—Martells and Hennessys

and Otards and the rest of them—echoed what was expressed forcefully by Heriard Dubreuil of the tiny family firm of Gautier Frères out at Aigre.[10]

'Double the vineyards, and we can double the sales'—it was almost like listening to, 'Give us the tools, and we'll finish the job.'

'Just look at the countryside—it's a scandal! No vineyards between here and Rouillac, yet it's *good* country: *premier cru*, Fins Bois!'

'*Premier cru*, Fins Bois, between here and Jarnac, too, and only the Bisquit vineyards—none for us smaller firms.'

The small growers and grower-distillers do not look at it in the same light—they fear that what the shippers are after is to bring down or, at any rate, to keep down prices.

'Ah,' said Gérard de Ramefort, at Otard, 'if only there were vertical integration! *That* would be a steadying influence. If only we shippers had bought vineyards when they were going cheap, after the phylloxera! But the tradition is that we shippers are the salesmen—we nearly all began as brokers or middlemen. We speculate in the product, but not in production.'

Trying to hold a balance between shipper and grower, the Government, advised by the Bureau National Interprofessionnel du Cognac, on which all interests are represented, and which is responsible to the Ministry of Agriculture, has given permission for another 50,000 acres of replanting over the next three years; increasing the existing acreage by about twenty-five per cent.

But it takes four to six years for a vine to bear; there will be a continuing shortage; stocks are low, which means that there is not enough cognac being aged.

Christian Braastad of Courvoisier was cynical where Monsieur de Ramefort of Otard was wistful. 'There are 250 shippers', he said, 'and 30,000 growers: it's a matter of voting power. Not that each grower wouldn't like to plant more vines, with prices what they are. But he doesn't want his neighbour to.'

Richard Roullet of Denis-Mounié talks in much the same strain: the farmer grows poor wine in the Charentes and as much

---

[10] This firm now belongs to the house of Berger, makers of the aperitif.

of it to the acre as he wants. In Bordeaux he produces good wine, and the law tells him how much he may grow. So although a grower of wine for cognac might only get a third the price for his wine that a claret grower gets, he can make five times as much to the acre. And who makes the wine into saleable cognac?

Meanwhile, the grower asks who will keep him and his family for the five years or so that a newly-planted vineyard is out of production—vine-growing is single-crop farming, the most hazardous of occupations: mixed farming is safer, and you can live on what you grow or rear. And look at the style the big shippers keep up, with their châteaux and their flats in Paris, their yachts and their racehorses!

* * *

Big changes are taking place in the world of cognac, and there will be more and bigger changes yet. The tensions between shippers and growers over replanting do nothing to spoil relations between this or that grower-distiller and the shipper he and his family have been selling to for generations, but it would be foolish to pretend that they do not exist.

Just as it would be to deny the difficulties that arose a year or so ago between shippers and between growers in the various zones—difficulties that were blown up by *Figaro* and other newspapers into '*la guerre du Cognac*'. It was more of a storm in a teacup, or a breeze in a brandy-glass, but it has its significance.

Rémy-Martin, having always made much, in addressing the British market, of producing nothing lower in quality than a VSOP, began also to make much of the fact, especially in their French publicity, that all their cognacs, whatever the quality, are blended only from the Grande and the Petite Champagnes, and thus entitled to the Fine Champagne *appellation*.

No one would mind—many firms make much of their Fines Champagnes. What upset other shippers, and among them the very biggest, was the suggestion that this is the only cognac worth having, and that hardly anyone but Rémy-Martin produces it.

The biggest houses in the trade, along with many others, have long believed that the brandy-drinker looks for a favourite

house or brand-name, not whether or not a cognac is or is not a
grande fine champagne.

Myself, I would go further. Who in this country calls at a bar
or at a restaurant table for a cognac? We ask for a brandy, and
we get a widely-advertised three-star. If we are asked, by barman
or wine-waiter, 'What kind of brandy?' we specify by name—
a Bisquit Dubouché perhaps or, indeed, a Rémy-Martin; a Hine
Antique or a Delamain Pale and Dry.

Hennessy, Martell and Courvoisier, leading critics of Rémy-
Martin, point out that between them they buy something like
seventy per cent of the Grande Champagne and Petite Champagne
crops, but still maintain that brandies from the other zones,
Borderies and Fins Bois, are needed to give style and character—
especially now that demand is making it necessary to sell younger
and younger blends: the Champagnes take longer than the
others to mature.

As a recent Martell brochure put it, prompted no doubt by the
Rémy-Martin advertising: 'To obtain a better quality [than that
of any one region] different cognacs, selected from among the
best . . . add each their own character—strength, body, mellowness, bouquet. Only in this manner can a "complete" cognac be
produced, possessing all the qualities which are rarely found
together in a single growth.'

I was in Cognac when *la guerre*, such as it was, was at its height,
and the Bureau National tried to tell me that it was not happening
or, if it were, why did I want to know about it? '*Il n'y a pas de
guerre de Cognac*', said Monsieur Coquillaud, its director-general,
in an interview with the local newspaper, which knew better;
and so the storm in a teacup looked more of a tempest than it
might otherwise have done. (How foolish official spokesmen are,
to pretend that certain conditions do not exist, certain incidents
have never happened! The journalist not only finds out, eventually, but inevitably magnifies the importance of what the spokes-
man has tried to hide: why did he try to hide it?)

It was enough of a war, at any rate, for a peace-treaty to
be signed: in April 1971, when leading shipping firms, Rémy-
Martin and the big three among them, met at the Bureau National
to sign a resolution, 'to end all opposition and disparaging

comments about the various crus'. The phrase is that of the covering letter from the big shipping firm that sent me a copy of the document.

What had been worrying many people in the trade was that prices of the Champagnes *crus* were being forced up by Rémy-Martin's publicity and buying policy. Not only did the other firms resent this, but growers and grower-distillers in the Borderies and the Fins Bois feared that *their* prices would correspondingly be forced down. There was a split in the growers' federation, and a breakaway body set up.

What *I* feared, if I may quote a typical lover of cognac, was that if other firms were pushed by one firm's insistence on its Fine Champagne into publicizing their house names as their strong selling points, why should they stick to the name of cognac at all? Would I know the difference if a Martell or a Hennessy three-star contained a percentage of grape brandy from outside the *appellation* area? Perhaps it would not matter, with firms as reputable as these: they would still make good brandy, and to their own house style. As I never asked for 'cognac' as such, anyway, but always for 'brandy', and then for a brand—it was all the same, wasn't it?

Well, no . . .

Trust the great old firms, by all means, but here would be thin ends of all sorts of wedges.

The very names of cognac and of Cognac have stood for quality for far longer than my lifetime: and for what is left of it I want the old-established houses to be as jealous of them as they always were and, praise be, still are.

Happily, the repercussions, as I write, have died down, and I may pick up my glass—not my big *ballon*, but my glass—of an early-landed, late-bottled cognac and sip it in peace, and at my ease.

I once boasted, years ago, in print, of having sat by the banks of the Charente and soothed my soul with a glass of brandy old enough to be my father. Such a cognac today, alas, would be woodier than I like: let it be one of my own age, which is old enough in all conscience, and echo the writer on cognac of the last century, who wrote:

'*L'aridité de notre description sera compensée, nous l'espérons, par le plaisir qu'aura le lecteur à savourer un verre de cognac, lorsqu'il saura par quelles phases est passé le liquide qu'il déguste.*'

I, too, hope that the dryness of the book will be dispelled by the pleasure in the glass.

Appendix I:

Extension of the Delimited Area

SINCE 1940 the area growing white wine for distillation into cognac has been extended, by permission, as follows. (The area is given in hectares: 1 hectare= approximately 2·5 acres.) About ninety per cent of the 1971 permitted area was actually in production.

Year	Area	Year	Area
1940	59,389	1956	63,062
1941	61,429	1957	61,603
1942	61,600	1958	62,596
1943	61,995	1959	64,114
1944	62,150	1960	68,693
1945	62,250	1961	69,608
1946	59,219	1962	70,646
1947	57,590	1963	72,616
1948	56,138	1964	75,452
1949	56,236	1965	78,491
1950	59,832	1966	81,058
1951	56,220	1967	81,187
1952	60,937	1968	82,372
1953	62,819	1969	82,500
1954	65,831	1970	82,734
1955	64,544	1971	86,243

Appendix I

This area is divided between the zones as follows:

Zones	Permitted area in production	Permitted area not in production	Total area
Grande Champagne	10,051	1,008	11,059
Petite Champagne	11,002	1,359	12,361
Borderies	3,151	341	3,492
Fins Bois	28,552	3,109	31,661
Bons Bois	19,244	1,704	20,948
Bois Ordinaires	6,411	311	6,722
Totals	78,411	7,832	86,243

Appendix II:

The Comparative Prices of Wine for Distillation

T HE cost to the distiller of wine for distillation is fixed each year by the Bureau National Interprofessional du Cognac, in general assembly, and is based in terms of Fins Bois at an arbitrary and notional coefficient of 100.

In 1972 the scale was:

Grande Champagne	114
Petite Champagne	107
Borderies	107
Fins Bois	100
Bons Bois	93
Bois Ordinaires	86

There are taxes to be added, other additions and, indeed, multiplications, and final prices are rounded up or down to the nearest five francs. There are small percentage allowances up and down for exceptional quality, or lack of it. But the scale gives an idea of the relative prestige of the six *crus*.

In the end, the price to the blender and shipper of new spirit distilled from these wines in 1972—spirit, that is, not yet one year old—was, per hectolitre at 100 degrees:

	francs
Grande Champagne	1,540
Petite Champagne	1,460
Borderies	1,460
Fins Bois	1,375
Bons Bois	1,295
Bois Ordinaires	1,210

Appendix III:

Sales of Cognac, 1947-48 to 1971-72, at Home and Abroad, Expressed in Hectolitres of Pure Alcohol

Year	Exported	France	Total
1947/1948	52,171	30,710	82,881
1948/1949	63,649	20,160	83,809
1949/1950	68,928	22,717	91,645
1950/1951	98,291	31,678	129,969
1951/1952	74,664	26,597	101,261
1952/1953	78,235	32,538	110,773
1953/1954	85,229	32,065	117,294
1954/1955	85,567	27,310	112,877
1955/1956	95,897	31,742	127,639
1956/1957	103,815	34,325	138,140
1957/1958	91,107	35,374	126,481
1958/1959	91,433	28,242	119,675
1959/1960	106,902	27,600	134,502
1960/1961	122,854	36,790	159,644
1961/1962	134,471	39,142	173,613
1962/1963	139,177	42,112	181,289
1963/1964	162,256	47,057	209,313
1964/1965	147,123	44,495	191,618
1965/1966	172,594	45,131	217,725
1966/1967	164,929	52,293	217,222
1967/1968	191,390	60,931	252,321
1968/1969	186,904	56,229	243,133
1969/1970	215,871	60,954	276,825
1970/1971	266,914	68,182	335,096
1971/1972	268,156	72,621	340,777

In the post-war period, the total sales of cognac have increased by more than 300 per cent, with exports increasing more than fivefold and the home trade following a slower but none the less steady rise,

It is of interest to note with reference to the total export quantity shown in the above analysis for the year 1971–72 that the distribution to the *principal* export markets was as follows (expressed in hectolitres of pure alcohol):

United Kingdom	52,521
West Germany	39,717
United States	27,098
Hong Kong	12,323
Holland	9,815
Malaysia & Singapore	9,410
Italy	8,561
Belgium	8,128
Switzerland	7,256
Finland	7,198
Canada	7,079
Denmark	4,993
Sweden	4,984
Norway	4,934
Ireland	4,587
Japan	4,520

Bibliographical Note

IT was a surprise to discover, when I began to plan this book, that there was no book on cognac in English.

Only half of T. A. Layton's slender *Cognac and Other Brandies* (London, 1968) concerns itself with cognac and, of that half, what is not an unacknowledged translation from French trade publications is inadequate and inaccurate.

The best general introductory sketch is still Delamain's *Histoire du Cognac* (Paris, 1935). The late Robert Delamain was not only a member of the Jarnac family long famous for the quality of its brandies, but also a man of letters. It is surprising that his short, well-written book was not Englished years ago: it outlines neatly the trade's structure and historical background, the methods of distilling and blending, and the charm of the Charentais countryside. Now, though, its manner dates it, and later historians have advanced theories more plausible than his as to how and why the region changed from vine-growing for wine to vine-growing for brandy.

By a happy chance, it was his kinsman, Alain Braastad-Delamain, a present director of the family firm, who gave me, some years ago, my copy of Roger Dion's *Histoire de la Vigne et du Vin en France* (Paris, 1959).

Professor Dion threw new light for me on the origins of the trade in cognac, and it will be evident from my chapter 3 how completely he has convinced me. It is a particular pleasure to me to record here my debt to a distinguished French scholar who is now an honorary vice-president of the British Circle of Wine Writers, of which I am president.

Another French historian whose work I have found invaluable is Gaston Tesseron, whose *La Charente sous Louis XIII* (Angoulême, 1955) and *La Charente sous Louis XIV*, vol. 1 (Angoulême, 1958) I consulted for the structure of the trade at those times. The second of these works was especially interesting on the great part that the Protestant community played in its development.

The works of Dion and Tesseron were all the more helpful in the absence of any serious work in English on our wine and spirit trade with France at this period.

André Simon's three-volume *History of the Wine Trade in England*, first published nearly seventy years ago, takes us only until 1703—when cognac was still a relative newcomer among our imports from the Charentes—and touches upon it only very little. I had high hopes of a book that appeared as

I was finishing my own, for it was entitled *The Wine Trade* and appeared in a scholarly-seeming series under a reputable imprint. But it turned out to be concerned almost entirely (and inaccurately) with our trade with the Iberian peninsula and, when remonstrated with, the publisher told me that, 'there simply would not have been room to do justice' to the wine trade with other countries. It should have had another title.

There is room for a serious continuation of Simon's pioneer work: the wine trade is no insignificant part of the economic history of this country.

References in L. Ravaz's *Le Pays du Cognac* (Angoulême, 1900) led me to dip into a number of nineteenth-century books in French that afforded sidelights and anecdotes, but none was either authoritative or exhaustive. G. Couanon's *Les Vins et Eaux-de-Vie de France* (Paris, 1921) and Pierre Vital's *Les Vieilles Vignes de Notre France* (Paris, n.d.: 1957?) were of similar limited use. I found interesting material in Lafon, *La Culture de la Vigne dans les Charentes* (Paris, 1912) on the relative merits of the Saint-Emilion and the Folle-Blanche grape.

On the laws relating to cognac and its *appellation* only the most serious scholar need consult Quittanson and Vanhouté's *La Protection des Appellations d'Origine et de la Commerce des Vins et Eaux-de-Vie* (Montpellier, 1963), for adequate summaries are provided in Marguerite Landrau's recent *Le Cognac Devant la Loi* (Montpellier, n.d.) and in *Le Cognac: Sa Distillation,* by R. Lafon, J. Lafon and Pierre Couillaud (Paris, 1964), which ranges more widely than its title suggests, and is as good a general survey as one could wish for of the techniques and structure of the trade. It includes an exhaustive bibliography of books in French.

Brief *Notes Pratiques sur la Distillation Charentaise* published by the Bureau Interprofessionnel summarize the methods of distillation itself, and add a much shorter list of recommended books.

* * *

Such use as I have made of more general works and of fiction will be evident from quotations in the text, and from footnotes, but I should make especial reference here again to Charles Morgan's novel *The Voyage,* set against the Jarnac of the time the phylloxera struck, and to J. A. Carnet's edition of Alfred de Vigny's *Lettres à Philipe Soulet et à Eugene Paignon* (Angoulême, 1965)—a sidelight not only on a Romantic poet as a practical *vigneron* and *bouilleur de cru,* but also on life in general and the cognac trade in particular in the Fins Bois of Louis Philippe's time and of the earlier years of the Second Empire.

Index